KU-017-670

Three Ways to Capsize a Boat

THREE WAYS TO CAPSIZE A BOAT

An Optimist Afloat

Chris Stewart

Sort Of
BOOKS

Acknowledgments

I'd like to thank Tom Cunliffe – and of course Ros and Hannah – for letting me
go with them to see the sea; Tim, for showing me the mountains of Greece;
Florika for much generosity and friendship; and Nat and Mark at Sort Of,
without whom the whole crazy episode would have been lost in the mists
of oblivion.

Three Ways to Capsize a Boat © 2009 by Chris Stewart. All rights reserved.
No part of this book may be reproduced in any form without permission from
the publisher except for the quotation of brief passages in reviews.

All photos in this book are © Tom Cunliffe. For information on Tom's own
books, DVDs and training, see www.tomcunliffe.com

Published in June 2009 by Sort Of Books, PO Box 18678, London NW3 2FL
www.sortof.co.uk

Distributed by the Profile/Independent Alliance and TBS in all territories
excluding the United States and Canada.

Typeset in Iowan Old Style BT , THE Sans and Vitrina to a design by Henry Iles.
Printed in the UK by Clays Ltd, Bungay, Suffolk.
192pp

A catalogue record for this book is available from the British Library.
ISBN 978-0-9560038-3-6

FSC
Mixed Sources
Product group from well-managed
forests and other controlled sources

Cert no. SGS - COC - 2061
www.fsc.org
© 1996 Forest Stewardship Council

Contents

PART ONE

Competent Crew

TEACH YOURSELF SAILING

IT WAS JULIE MILLER WHO SENT ME TO SEA, one wet autumn afternoon on the Wandsworth Road. Now of course you haven't a clue who Julie Miller is – why should you? – but her relevance to this episode is that she had a great aunt called Jane Joyce.

'Chris!' yelled Julie, who was more than a match for the thundering of London traffic, 'What a fantastic coincidence. I've been longing to see you and there is something I particularly wanted to ask you... what was it now? Ah yes, how would you like a job looking after a yacht in the Greek Islands this summer?'

'I'd like that very much,' I replied, without so much as a thought. 'As it happens I'm not too busy this summer.' Which was the long and the short of it, for at the tender age of twenty-nine my career as a sheep farmer had just hit the skids. The bank had refused any further loans to nurture the flock that my girlfriend, Ana, and I were tending on rented land in Sussex, and my 'prospects', as my mother insisted on calling them, were not looking overly bright.

'Terrific,' said Julie. 'That's a very great relief. My Great-Aunt Jane has been on at me for weeks to find her a skipper, and I thought of you straight away.'

Now this, it must be said, was a most peculiar thing to think. For I had never been on a boat before in my life, and I knew not the first thing about sailing. But I desperately wanted a job, so it struck me that it might be best to keep minor details like this to myself.

CLEARLY, THE FIRST THING TO DO was to bone up on boating, in order to conduct myself satisfactorily at the interview. So I bought *Teach Yourself Sailing* or some such guide and immersed myself in it. It was not, I thought, quite as gripping as a book on such an interesting subject ought to be, and I emerged from it with only the haziest notions. If I had the pictures in front of me I could tell the difference between a sloop (gaff-rigged or Bermuda), a schooner, a ketch and a yawl; I had a very vague idea what beating and tacking and running were; I had learnt the undesirability of gybing when running; and I could tell you more or less when to reef, or if things cut up really rough, to scandalise.

I did a little work on the vocabulary, too. I discovered that ropes were not actually ropes, but sheets, lines, halyards, warps, painters, stays or ratlines. The toilet was not the dunny but the heads. Of course the front wasn't the front and the back wasn't the back.... then there was a fid and the bitts and take-alls, there were peaks, luffs and clews, and if you didn't feel too good you could always heave to.

Friends and family were concerned about my cavalier attitude and horribly obvious ignorance. 'What if you tip the old bird into the drink?' they asked. 'How would you live with yourself if you (1) drowned the lot of them, (2) wrecked the boat, and (3) killed yourself in the process?'

I pointed out the tautology, reassured them that things would turn out for the best, and dialled the number of my patron-to-be. A pleasingly patrician American voice answered.

'But my dear, I have been simply longing for you to ring. Dear Julie has told me all about you and I simply cannot wait to meet you in the flesh, so to speak. However, things being as they are, I suppose I shall have to. So perhaps Tuesday evening at eight o'clock would suit you?'

I returned my nose to the sailing book and tested myself one more time on vocabulary – full and by, gybing, reaching, tacking... goose wing, veering, backing. Then, got up like a dog's dinner – I think I even wore a tie – I rang the bell at two minutes to eight at a very opulent brick apartment block in Cadogan Square. A tall, slightly stooped octogenarian opened the door. He had thick white hair, a bulbous nose, and spoke quietly in a voice that was full of slowness and gentleness.

'Why, you must be Chris.' He offered me his hand, which I shook as firmly as I thought proper for one so frail. 'Welcome. Come in. I'm Bob Joyce, but please call me Bob. Jane will be down shortly. In the meantime, perhaps you'd care for a drink.'

'I'll have a whisky and soda...' I replied. It seemed the right drink for a captain, though I can't remember ordering the drink from choice on any other occasion.

'Very sensible too. Ice?'

'Er, yes, please.'

Bob busied himself at the drinks cabinet. I took stock of my surroundings – immense but rather gloomy opulence.

'Yes, you're right, it is a little on the tenebrous side, but we've only taken it for a few months – and at least it's warm.' Funny, I hadn't said anything. 'Here, have a seat, Chris. I believe you're to be our skipper this summer?'

'Yes that's right, or rather I hope so.'

'Well I hope so, too, Chris. Cheers. It's no good talking to me about boats though; I hate the damn things. The boat is my wife's hobby.'

A rustle of expensive materials, a scent of gardenias and Jane was down.

'Chris, how good of you to come. I am charmed to meet you. Now Bobby, have you given our skipper a drink? Yes, good, I see you have. Please sit down.'

Jane was a whirlwind of a woman, getting on for seventy, I supposed, but still quite a beauty, and with an air of ease and power. I fumbled for something nautical to say but, hell, we didn't want to get into all that stuff about heads and bitts just yet. Jane was running the show, anyway. Bob sipped his whisky and drummed his fingers on his knee.

Jane poured herself a drink and sat down opposite me, looking at me keenly as she made her assessment.

'Chris, I feel sure we shall get along wonderfully well; your references are impeccable. I won't even tell you what Julie said about you – and Julie is a person whose opinions I take very seriously. Now, I imagine you know all there is to know about sailing, so we needn't bother ourselves with that...'

Idiotically, I failed to take this easy escape route. My brain was still in sailing mode, and I was desperately trying to come up with something which would give Jane the impression that I was a nautical sort of a person.

'Is... is she a gaffer?' I spluttered.

'I beg your pardon, my dear?'

'I mean the boat, the yacht... is she a gaffer?'

'Is she a what?' Her face took on a rather pained expression.

'A gaffer – you know, gaff-rigged...'

'I haven't the faintest idea, Chris. Does it matter?'

'No – no, not at all, just curiosity. I'd sort of like to know what manner of boat I'll be sailing.'

'Well, I'll tell you what I'll do. I'll send you the brochure and everything else, all the details before you come.'

This was a piece of cake, like taking candy from a baby. Bob poured me another whisky while Jane filled me in on my duties. My pay would be fifty pounds a week plus a living allowance. I would collect the boat from where it was moored at a marina near Athens, and sail it down to the island of Spetses, and there we would spend the summer. I would start in May, to get the boat ready for the Joyces' arrival. Jane, in spite of the apparent grace of her carriage, was about to undergo a double hip transplant. The summer sailing season would start as soon as she recovered from the operation.

And that was that. I had passed the interview – albeit as the only applicant. Which, thinking about it, is really my preferred sort of interview. All of a sudden I was a Greek island yacht skipper, with a bigger pay packet than I'd ever had before, and a long summer of sunshine and sailing before me. My ship, you might say, had come in.

I skipped ecstatically across Battersea Bridge, to where I was staying with my sister. And as I skipped, the first cloud of doubt began to form. From what I had seen of these Joyces, I liked them; and they were family to some cherished friends of mine. Perhaps my critics were right, and it was time I started to take this business a little more seriously.

When I returned to Sussex, I took Ana to our local pub and told her about my amazing good fortune. Now, as luck would have it, there was, drinking in the pub at the time, a man called Keith, who had for some months been trying to worm his way into the favours of Ana. I remember him as a rather malodorous person with a black beard, a boyish, chubby face, and not the remotest snowball in hell's chance of making it with my woman, because – apart from anything else – he was too damn mean even to buy a round of drinks.

I was crowing to him about my exciting windfall when he stopped me and said: 'It so happens that I've just bought my first boat. She's moored at Littlehampton and I don't have a car, so if you drive me down to the boat, I'll give you a sailing lesson.'

We cemented the pact with a beer… which I bought.

THIS WAY, THEN THAT

A FEW DAYS LATER, on a bone-chilling misty April morning, I found myself on the dock at Littlehampton, watching while Keith buggered about with what appeared to me meaningless and boring preparations for the forthcoming voyage. His boat was a bit of a disappointment, too – a grotty little twenty-one-foot craft banged together out of plywood and tin. It had the advantage, though, he told me, of being extremely cheap. She was called, whether coincidentally or not, *Ana*, and this set me to wondering just what sort of hideous designs Keith had on my girlfriend. Still, you don't look a gift horse in the mouth... and you certainly didn't want to look Keith in the mouth; his halitosis, poor boy, could drop a man at fifty feet. He worked for the DHSS.

After an eternity of fidgeting about with ropes and a bucket, Keith started the outboard motor. 'Pibble pibble

ibble obble ibble obble,' it went. We slipped the mooring lines and pottered out into the river, then down past the pier and out into the high sea. I stood half frozen by the mast, thinking of Odysseus leaving Ithaca, and trying to look important and knowledgeable.

Two minutes after passing the head of the pier we were surrounded by mist. I forgot Odysseus and started to think of the Ancient Mariner. This, then, must be the sea, I thought. It was calm, with just a faintly disagreeable heaving about it, and you couldn't see a thing. I shivered. Keith turned the engine off, which was a blessing as the sound it made was extremely irritating. Silence... apart from the slop of the waves against the side of the boat, and the drip, drip of the water condensing on the rigging.

'Right,' said Keith excitedly. 'Time to get the sails up.'

I went below, where it was even more unpleasant than above, and passed the sails out to Keith. Then, with a mild feeling of nausea I helped him unfold them and fix them to the various shackles and stays. This was good, as it engaged me in meaningful occupation for a minute or two. We hoisted the sails, made fast their ropes and, with Keith taking the tiller, sat back to watch what happened.

'We're sailing!' cried Keith, beside himself with excitement. I couldn't see it myself; as far as I could gather we were just bobbing up and down in a great wet white bowl of nothingness. It was chilly and damp and I was thinking to myself that perhaps I had made a terrible mistake, because if this was sailing, then I didn't like it, not one little bit.

'Look, we're actually making headway, we're bowling along,' shouted Keith in an excess of misplaced euphoria. I licked my finger and held it up to see if I could detect any breeze, cat's paw, zephyr or other sign of movement. Nothing. He pulled the tiller over and shouted the words, 'Ready about... LEE HO!' I stared at him incredulously. What sort of instruction was that for one sensible adult to shout at another?

The boom swung gently towards us. It seemed we were supposed to duck under it and shuffle onto the other side of the cockpit, keeping the ropes in hand as we went. The boat apparently swung round but, although we were now ostensibly facing a different direction nothing else seemed to have changed. Actually, it was impossible to be sure where you were facing, as the closeness of the thick white fog had a peculiarly disorientating effect. I no longer knew where the shore was, even though it couldn't have been as much as a hundred yards off.

We ate our cheese and tomato sandwiches in silence, more as a way of relieving the monotony than because we were hungry. In a desultory fashion I read bits of my book about sailing, but if the truth be told, I was going off it fast. For most of that long, gloomy April day we went bobbing first this way, then that, in the middle of nowhere. Occasionally we would drag a finger in the water to see if we could perceive any sign of movement. The fog sat heavy on the sea and refused to lift. From somewhere came the mournful whoo-ing of a foghorn buoy and the half-hearted clank of a bell. This was just about as depressing as a thing could be.

Finally Keith, too, decided that he'd had enough. He started the engine and we turned to where he reckoned the pier was. We were actually a fair way off; I suppose the tide must have taken us. The fog lifted just a little bit and we could see in the distance the pier that ran out from the mouth of the river. Slowly, unbelievably slowly, we approached it. I could hardly believe how slow our progress was. It took us the best part of an hour to cover what must have been less than a quarter of a mile, and the closer we got to it, the slower our rate of approach seemed to be. As we puttered beyond the lighthouse on the end of the breakwater an ordinary garden snail could have given us a run for our money.

We moved on up the river – the dock was still about a half a mile off – our progress becoming feebler and feebler. Keith wound the little outboard up to maximum power, a horrible high-pitched scream. Now we were in the river we were making even less headway, for the tide was ripping down here at full bore. All the ditches and streams and rivers of rain-sodden Sussex were pouring their turgid waters into the Arun, and the Arun was hurling them down against us and our poor desperate little boat, along with a thousand million tons of seawater that had somehow got mixed up in the equation.

Finally we stopped moving altogether, although if you looked over the side of the boat at the wake, it appeared we were thundering along. I took a sight on a couple of posts on either side of the pier, and realised that with all the effort of that screaming overheating engine we were moving not one inch. The day's sailing had been boring in a quiet sort of way; this part was also boring but with the screaming of the engine to make it worse. There was a sense of humiliation too; we felt a pair of utter berks, completely immobile but with the motor giving it all it had got.

People strolled out along the pier to have a look at us. They would lean on the wet railings and consider us for a few minutes, perhaps even point us out to the kids or give a wave, while we did our best to preserve some dignity and look as if we were in command of the situation. Eventually boredom would set in and they'd disappear, perhaps to have tea in the tearoom. But an hour later they'd be back. The river of course was still raging past us, so we'd be exactly where we were before, and they'd greet us again with unfeigned surprise and enthusiasm, waving as if to old friends. We must have looked a ridiculous sight.

We were stuck in that river for the best part of two hours – two of the longest hours I've ever known. But at last a powerful fishing-boat came up beside us, and a fisherman, a big man with a lot of condensation and what looked like bits of fish in his beard, leaned over with a grin and asked us if we wanted a tow. We did. He threw us a line and set off upriver.

Keith was at the back holding the tiller. I was on the fore-deck, holding the rope and wondering just what to do with it. 'Quick, pass it through the fairleads and hitch it round the bitts,' he yelled. What the hell was a fairlead? And I couldn't for the life of me remember what or where the bitts was.

I looked at him uncomprehendingly, as the slack in the rope snaked out over the edge of the boat.

'Alright then...' Keith was beside himself now. 'Just take it and cleat it off round the bitts.'

I didn't know what the hell he meant, could hardly hear him above the screaming engine. Surely he hadn't said, 'Take it and beat it off round the clitts!'? I sniggered to myself at this rich notion – and the rope snapped taut, nearly heaving me bodily off the front of the boat. But somehow I kept my balance and held on grimly, squatting on the foredeck like a downhill skier crouched for speed. We moved up the river, the fishermen shaking their heads in disbelief.

Round the corner and we were beside the dock. The current was a little slacker here as the river was wider. The fishermen waved us goodbye and I dropped the rope into the water. Keith steered us nervously to the dock with the screaming engine. 'Prepare the warps!' he yelled.

I looked around. What the hell were the warps and where were they?

'Alright, you take the tiller and I'll do the warps; just steer us into that dock over there.'

I stumbled to the back of the boat while Keith staggered to the bow. I took the tiller, happy at last to be doing the fun bit. I eased in towards the dock and gave a professional sort of a blip to the throttle... whereupon the engine stopped.

Keith spun round, tripped on a warp and with a foul oath fell overboard. One moment he was there; next moment he was gone. I heard a mad scrabbling, a splash and then... just the rocking of the boat.

For a brief moment, I wondered if I should try and rescue Keith, but as the boat was now spinning in the current, all set to rocket back down the river and out to sea, I couldn't see there was much I could do. Poor Keith: I hoped he was alright and had managed to thrash his way to the shore – though there didn't seem much point in dwelling on such matters. I pulled the starter rope on the engine... nothing.

'Chris!' There came a strangled croak.

'Yes, what?'

'Help me back on board, you arsehole!'

'Thank God, Keith!' I exclaimed, peering over the side. 'You really had me worried there!' And with a lot of undignified heaving and grunting I started to pull the poor sodden bloke back onto the boat – no easy matter as he was on the big side anyway and, with the wool of his clothes having absorbed a couple of bucketfuls of river water, he must have weighed about as much as an average walrus. This operation inevitably resulted in the loss of much valuable time, and although the tide had slackened off a bit, by the time the poor shivering Keith had got the engine restarted we were shooting out sideways past the end of the pier again.

This time it only took us about forty-five minutes to cover the half-mile back to the dock. Keith filled the time usefully with an exhaustive explanation of the procedures with the warps and the whole business of docking, and when we got there it went smoothly, without a hitch.

After a long and tedious episode during which Keith beavered about making the boat 'shipshape', as he insisted on calling it, we had a beer in the yacht club and discussed the lessons we had learned. I had had no inkling of the danger Keith was in – nor the boat, nor myself, for that matter. It seemed to me that if you fell in a river you swam to the bank and got out, simple as that. I had not taken into account the awesome power of the tides – and this on a little river like the Arun. I was inclined to treat the whole thing as a laugh; it had certainly been a lot more fun than the so-called sailing we had been doing earlier.

All in all we got off lightly. Keith's boat didn't get wrecked; he didn't drown, and I learned a thing or two about sailing, although perhaps not as much as I should have done. I fear I am a rather obtuse person.

IT MAY SEEM ODD TO YOU that either Keith or I would ever want to sail with one another again – but we did, the following weekend. This time there was actually some wind, and with it, or rather against it, we sailed all the way to Chichester harbour, most of the trip being in the dark.

This is one of the things that I was learning about sailing: it wasn't just a matter of going when the mood took you,

you had to take into account the tides. This more often than not involved leaving in the middle of the night or, worse still, just before the onset of night, so that just as you got out into the sea you would be enveloped by an intimidating and unhelpful blackness. I comforted myself with the thought that in the Mediterranean everything would be simpler, as the tides are negligible, so we would be able to go wherever and whenever we wanted.

Here, though, we were confronted by dark and empty distances, filled only by the stars, the little light on our compass, and a constellation of far-off winking lights that, according to Keith, were telling us where to go. Once again I had little idea of the dangers of sailing, especially on a boat with a person like Keith. And as far as he was concerned I was a menace. However, perhaps as a consequence of his halitosis and his parsimony, he was not exactly inundated with eager applicants.

The dangers became all too apparent the next day when we attempted to return from Chichester. We were about a mile off the beach at Climping when the weather turned truly nasty. The wind began to howl and soon whipped the sea into a convoluted mass of raging waves and every way we looked there were immense walls of grey-green water, capped by dirty white foam with skeins of spray coming off the top. The roar of rolling and breaking water and the shrieking of the wind made it impossible to think straight. We both wore oilskins but even so we were sopping with salty water, and only the busy-ness of staying alive kept us from feeling the hellish cold. The little boat was tossed from trough to peak and Keith and I were hurled about like ninepins in a skittle alley.

I was on the tiller with a handful of sheets (the ropes that control the sails) and Keith was up on the front frantically tying up great folds of sail. I was all for scandalising the main – and as it happened, given the way things turned out, it wouldn't have been a bad thing to do. For suddenly all hell broke loose as we were hit by a gust of wind like a battering ram. There wasn't much of us in the water anyway as a result of being hurled into the air at that same moment by a colossal wave, and the next thing I knew Keith and I were thrashing about in the furious sea, and the boat upside down, with its keel (the fin that ought to be at the bottom) on top.

There was a brief moment of shock, then the icy cold water flooded into my oilskins, making me catch my breath and start to sink. The water was cold enough to seize up all my muscles but the sudden imperative of keeping afloat in order to gulp the next breath kept me moving. Curiously, I also recall hooting with watery laughter – which with hindsight must have been the beginnings of some sort of hysteria.

I still had little idea of what was at stake, though. When we bobbed to the top of a wave I could see the white foaming breakers on the beach about a mile away. I thought we could always swim if the worst came to the worst. I've never actually swum a mile, and certainly not wearing oilskins nor in a cold, rough sea. Keith told me later that we wouldn't have stood a chance, indeed that it was little short of a miracle that we had survived. And in no uncertain terms he made clear that it was my fault that we had capsized. I had unaccountably hung onto the sheet, instead of letting it fly.

However, then and there, Keith appeared in his best colours as he showed me how to stand on the keel of the boat and pull it back upright again. This was a a lot harder than it sounds, because by this time *Ana* was completely full of water. However, as a result of titanic effort and a big helping of luck, the dear little boat righted herself, and after a protracted struggle to get ourselves back on board we set course with sodden charts, bailing all the way, for Littlehampton.

It took about six hours of teeth-chattering, waterlogged misery, but when we got to the dock we felt pretty good – as if we had been somewhere where not many others had been... and I don't mean Chichester Harbour.

Dear Keith, I quite liked him in the end, and I wish him all the best, and hope that he finally found an Ana of his own, and that the watery grave that looked to me like it might be his lot hasn't yet claimed him.

SARK BY STARLIGHT

I HAD DECIDED BY THIS TIME, as any sane person might, that I hated sailing and didn't want anything further to do with it. However, I had given my word to Julie's great-aunt that I would skipper her boat, and I didn't like the idea of admitting my deceit, or letting her down. Besides, I didn't have any other job prospects on the immediate horizon. So, scraping together a little money from some sheep-shearing work, I enrolled at the Isle of Wight Sailing School. I was signed up for a fortnight's course that would give me a certificate as a 'Competent Crew' and then 'Day Skipper'.

I wasn't thrilled at the prospect of any kind of school, and had pretty much made up my mind that sailing was either dangerous or boring, or more often both. Still, I'd paid my money, so I had no option but to make the best of a bad job. I took the train down to Portsmouth and then caught the ferry across to Cowes.

We – the hopeful competent crew – were divided four to a boat and assigned a skipper-teacher who would arrive the following morning. My crew were an odd mix: Roger, an Indian property developer from north London; Suzie, a plump, pretty primary school teacher; and Simon, a police inspector from Bognor who was learning to sail, he said, to fill his Sundays since his wife left him.

In the morning our skipper arrived, an enormous man, seemingly made from a different mould to the rest of us. His physical immensity – he was six feet six and built like a heap of bricks – barely hinted at the enormousness of his presence. Tom Cunliffe was his name and I gathered that he was something of a big cheese (or whatever is the correct nautical term) in the sailing world. He was a serious long-distance sailor and had navigated most of the seas and oceans of the world on merchant ships or yachts. He was a most artistic user of English, with language gleaned in equal measure from Shakespeare and the mess-rooms of tramp steamers. He could be filthy when he felt like it, but you couldn't take offence because of his artistry and his big-hearted good humour. He was funny, too, and would have you rolling about and clutching your sides. Tom quite took the wind from my sails... so to speak.

Competent Crew was a simple, undemanding course; we learned the vocabulary of sailing and what everything was for and why. We learned a dozen different knots and why it's important to get them right. To flake and coil ropes we learned too, and when Tom demonstrated, the rope seemed to come alive in his huge hands.

'And that', he would boom, 'is the way to do a first-class Flemish Flake.'

We did a little basic navigation and some sailing theory. Then we took on a box of provisions for the week and slipped away down the river into the Solent.

It was a seascape unrecognisable from my adventures with Keith. The sea was blue and the sun shone, and with a gentle breeze the boat went bounding across the water like a happy dog. We moored one night in the beautiful Beaulieu river. We took the dinghy across the quiet water to the pub at Buckler's Hard, where Tom sang sea shanties with the band. And in the morning we woke with thick heads, to the silence of the still river amongst the woods, and the haunting cries of seabirds. And then we battled against the wind and the waves, bashing our way through the flying spray to tie up at Bosham in Chichester Harbour.

The next week we sailed overnight to the island of Sark and I learned the pleasure of sailing by the stars in the open sea. As we approached the island, because we'd been a day and a night at sea and our sense of smell was hankering for the land, the flowering gorse all over the island scented the sea for miles around. Tom was an inspiration; he loved the sea and knew how to inspire others with that love.

At the end of the week, proudly clutching my certificates, I felt I had just tasted a tiny smattering of something that would haunt me to the end of my days. I was almost feeling a sense of destiny and recalled that my grandfather on my father's side, who had died before I was born, had been a captain. He had ferried captured German battleships back to Britain after the First World War. So maybe this was in my blood. I felt more than ready for the isles of Greece.

PART TWO

The Isles of Greece

WHERE IS WEARE?

WHEN I GOT HOME there was a package for me from Jane Joyce. It contained a letter explaining the way things stood, a letter of introduction to a certain Captain Bob Weare, and a brochure with details of the boat, as well as a receipt for a sum of money she had paid the said captain.

'I am about to go under the knife,' she wrote. 'Meanwhile here is what you must do. The boat is not at the island, Spetses, yet. It has been looked after this winter by Captain Bob, who I fear is a dreadful old reprobate. He has the papers and the keys and has undertaken some repairs that had become necessary. He can be contacted at Bar Thalassa, Euripides 5, Kalamaki. Goodbye, my dear, the best of luck and I look forward to seeing you and the refurbished Crabber in Spetses on my return.' There was also a cheque for a couple of hundred dollars to cover expenses.

I looked at the pictures of my first command, a pretty little boat with a long wooden bowsprit and a picturesque suit of red canvas sails... a long way from a captured battleship, but it would do for a start.

I FLEW TO ATHENS AND TOOK A BUS down to Kalamaki, where, humping my bag and my guitar with me, I trudged round the hot streets looking for Euripides. 'Thalassa' means 'sea' in Greek, so I figured the bar must be on the waterfront. But it wasn't, and after a number of confusions and misdirections, I eventually tracked it down. It was a dreary sort of a dive, with plastic tables perched on the kerb of a back street, beneath some stunted plane trees, but the barman was pleasant, spoke some English and knew my man.

Captain Bob, it seemed, was in the habit of coming to the bar at about six or seven, though he hadn't been seen for some days. I stowed my baggage in a corner of the bar and, ordering a salad and a jug of retsina, sat in the shade with my Greek grammar. Customers came and went, flies buzzed, cars and vans crawled along the potholed road. Six o'clock came and went, so did seven and eight o'clock. The sun set, and with it came the blessed cool of evening and the orange glow of street lights; my Greek book was becoming increasingly tedious. With no sign of Captain Bob, I checked into a hotel recommended by the barman, conveniently located just beneath the take-off path of the airport, a cheap dump of a place that turned out, with the inevitability of these things, to be a whorehouse.

Next day I returned to Thalassa for breakfast and afterwards headed down to the marina to see if I could find the boat. There were hundreds and hundreds of gleaming plastic boats all bobbing at their moorings on the foul, oily slop that constituted the sea in Kalamaki Marina. In the hot morning sun I marched along pontoon after pontoon, watching the glistening brown men and women beavering about on their boats. But there was nothing even remotely resembling a Cornish Crabber.

It wasn't hard to tell, as a Crabber is a most singular design of boat. From the brochure that Jane Joyce had sent me I knew that the hull was black; that her mast and spars were wooden as opposed to the more modern aluminium; that her sails were red and her stem was plumb... and sure as hell she would be the only boat in all of Kalamaki Marina with a plumb stem. (A plumb stem is where the front of the boat or bow enters the waterline at the vertical, as opposed to the elegant streamlined curve of, say, a clipper stem. It's the way fishing smacks are, and all the boats that feature in eighteenth- and nineteenth-century Dutch seascape paintings have plumb stems.)

All in all the Crabber was the choice of an aesthetically sophisticated lady owner who knew nothing about sailing but was determined that it should be beautiful. There was no sign, though, of such a boat amongst the slinky white craft moored stern to (parked backwards) at the pontoons.

Next I checked the area where the boats were lined up in winter storage – again nothing resembling a Crabber. Finally, a little confused and worried, I went across to a sort of dump where the wrecks lay, poor old crippled boats who had given of their best and were now left to rot in this dusty corner of the boatyard. There were scores of boats here; I walked up and down the lines and in and out between them and suddenly, emerging from behind a rusting steel hulk, I saw the Crabber. There was no mistaking it. She was listing to one side, half propped by some flimsy timbers and with a tattered tarpaulin half on and half off.

I didn't know a lot about boat maintenance then, but this poor old thing was in the most terrible state. It was quite clear that nobody had done a stitch of work on it all winter. It was a wreck. I climbed on board and looked it over. There wasn't even an engine in it – the removal of which seemed to be about as far as the winter maintenance had gone. I sat there in the hot sun on the boat and studied the battered woodwork. It didn't take much to see that the famous Captain Bob was a crook, or an incompetent, or both.

I spent another afternoon in the bar trying hard to concentrate on my Greek grammar, but more often contemplating what looked like the ruin of my promising summer. There was no sign of Weare. I wondered how Jane, with all her apparent competence and authority, had been gulled by this person who had neither address nor phone number, but just a bar as a point of contact. But then again, she had contracted me as skipper and sent me a cheque for the boat's expenses. Perhaps she was a little too trusting.

IT WAS MORE THAN A WEEK before I managed to run Captain Weare to ground.

One evening I entered the Thalassa as usual, a little angry by now and far from confident of meeting the person whose deceitfulness was laying waste my plans for the summer. But on this occasion Yannis, the waiter, beckoned me over.

'Weare is here,' he said in an undertone, flicking his eyes towards an outside table. 'There is Weare.'

Apprehensively I went over to the table, where the man was drinking a beer with some associates. 'Would you be Captain Weare?' I asked, making an effort to be polite and unaggressive.

He half turned and looked at me without warmth for a moment, before saying, 'Who wants him?'

Weare, seated in his chair, was a short, stout man with no apparent neck. His face was a shocking red and dominated by a round and pockmarked nose and eyes of a watery and unlovely blue. He wore a filthy white boiler suit.

I extended my hand, which he shook perfunctorily.

'My name's Chris,' I said. 'And I'm looking after the Crabber this summer for Jane Joyce.'

He considered me arrogantly, then took a swig from his beer. 'You are, are you?' he said. 'Well the boat's not ready yet; there's some finishing touches left to do.'

'I should think there are,' I said, struggling to contain myself. 'It hasn't even got the engine in...'

'The engine', sneered Weare, 'is the least of its problems. It's got osmosis.'

It was becoming increasingly difficult to keep my temper, but the bastard held all the trump cards – he knew the boat and, more to the point, had the engine, keys and papers.

'So what do you intend to do about it?' I spluttered.

'Know about osmosis, then, do you?' he asked, as he reached for the beer again and with his eyes fixed on mine took another long swig.

I stammered something incoherent about this not being the issue.

'Look,' he growled, 'I haven't time to explain it all to you tonight.' And he turned his back to me and spat some words out in Greek. From his friends' raucous laughter I could tell they were obscenities.

Quaking with fury, I went to pay my bill at the bar. 'I tell you what Bob Weare is like,' said Yannis, with a look of complicity. 'He is of bad character.'

I went to a phone box and rang Jane in London.

'Chris,' she said. 'I've always had my suspicions of this man, and from what you say I now doubt that he was ever a captain of anything. The title is mere mendacity. You have my full confidence and authority to do what needs to be done. I am so sorry for your trouble. It is entirely my fault for putting my trust in this serpent. I promise I will make it up to you, but now, if you will, I would like you to take the matter out of the detestable Weare's hands, arrange to have done whatever work needs to be done to the boat, and sail her down to the island.'

There was something about the sincerity with which she issued this trusting and near impossible demand that seduced me utterly. At that moment I would have laid down my life for her. Certainly I would take on the task of sorting out the beastly machinations of the serpent Weare. But it would be far from easy, as I knew nothing of Greece, my command of the language was negligible, and I had never fixed up a boat before. On top of which there was Weare to contend with, and as the days went by he seemed to do everything in his power to make things even more difficult than they already were.

I had imagined that by now I would be living on the boat in the pretty little harbour of Spetses, and that my days would be spent cruising pleasantly from island to island with my enchanting employer and her friends. Instead I was stuck in Kalamaki, one of the vilest spots in Greece, where the roar of the constant traffic on the busy coastal road to Athens was smothered every ten minutes or so throughout the day and night by the noise of aircraft taking off and landing. There was a long, grubby beach on the edge of the road and a line of enormous ugly hotels.

The marina itself was vast, and all the more galling for me as I watched boat after boat set off from the harbour mouth into the beautiful blue sea beyond. They were like flying ants, launching themselves one after another from a blade of grass, and me the poor earthbound ant, condemned to stay behind, wingless, and watch them, as the sun caught and then flickered in the beauty of their silver wings.

The only consolation – and there always is a consolation – was a patisserie half an hour's walk away in the town. Here I would sit at the end of the day, and with the joy of Nikos Kazantzakis's *Zorba the Greek* – I had dumped the grammar – assuage the misery of my situation with a coffee and the most divine chocolate cake, or perhaps a mango ice cream. It is one of life's great blessings that the safety valves of the human condition operate in such a simple way: misery's turmoil sweetly stilled by a sip of fine wine; pain dulled by a bite of good bacon, or a smile from a pretty girl.

Little by little I made progress, too. I travelled on foot in the heat and the dust from one yacht chandler to another until I found somebody prepared, for a consideration, to help me sort my problem out. I hit upon a person who I reckoned was called Ecstaticos, although I was told later that it was Eustathios. He was a smooth operator if ever I saw one, in a sharp suit and shades, and with a glinting smile, but at least he was prepared to take the job on. 'My men will be there tomorrow morning,' he assured me as we sat in his opulent air-conditioned office in Piraeus. 'They will assess the problem and do the work and you will have your boat.'

I shook hands with him, and bounced off to ring the Boss. As a result of being so steeped in *Zorba*, I had taken to calling Jane 'Boss', which she seemed to like.

'We're on the move, Boss,' I cried joyously down the phone. 'Work starts tomorrow morning and I guess I'll be bringing the boat down sometime next week.'

'Well, hot lickety dogspittle, I knew all along you were the man for the job. Well done, dear Chris, and thank you, thank you.'

A WEEK LATER, as I waited disconsolately and alone on the wreck of my summer command, a disreputably shabby old three-wheeled tin van, which the Greeks call a *trikiklo*, wormed its way among the potholes, rusting iron and nautical detritus of the Kalamaki boat graveyard. I watched it with interest, and the smallest shred of hope kindling in my heart. It pulled up uncertainly. The incumbents extricated themselves from the little cab and looked up at me.

'You Jane Joyce?' said the shorter of the two, squinting against the sunlight.

'No, I'm Chris.'

'I'm Nikos.'

We shook hands. The other one emerged from the other side of the boat, which he had been inspecting.

'Hi,' he said – they both spoke English with a strong transatlantic accent – 'Nikos.'

'You're both Nikos, then?'

'Yup,' they chorused. Not that you could confuse the two of them: one was tall and dark with an aquiline nose, the other slight with a close red beard.

'Y'know, Chris,' said red-beard-Nikos, 'I would say that this ain't so much a yacht like we was led to believe, more a boat, no?'

While he was making this observation tall-dark-Nikos was dragging a heap of junk, that might once have been tools, out of the *trikiklo*. 'Right, let's look see what we gonna do.'

They crawled all over the boat, poked it and tapped it and scraped it and confabulated unfathomably in Greek.

'Got some osmosis and it don' seem to have no engine,' announced red-beard-Nikos. 'The engine we can get a noo engine an' put 'er in, the osmosis we gotta take the whole outer coatin' of the hull off and give 'er another coat. Then we oughta clean up the spars a bit an' touch up the wood-work... take about a week, I guess.'

A week... just a week! The scales of gloom dropped from my heart and I skipped inwardly with sweetest delight. Ana was coming over for a holiday in a week – and the thought of having the Crabber to cruise her round the Greek islands... well, I could scarcely contain my happiness.

And then I remembered I didn't have the boat's keys. I put this to the Nikoses.

'Keys, man?' laughed tall-dark-Nikos. 'Keys are for engines. You got no engine. We get a noo engine, noo keys. No problem.' And having sprung me free in one simple phrase from the hold Weare had over me, he pulled the cord and started the generator. Each Nikos then connected up an angle grinder and laid into the hull.

I was jubilant and would have gambolled like a lamb and sung like a lark except that the whining and screaming of the grinders and the evil-smelling black dust of vaporised paint and glass fibre were choking out every impulse. The sun had risen and was hot as hell, too. But the Nikoses were young and tough and it seemed like they knew what they were at.

'You wanna grinder?' asked tall-dark-Nikos.

'Sure, if it'll make things quicker.' I tied a handkerchief over my nose and mouth in imitation of my new friends, and got stuck into the other side of the hull. It was an awful job, the noise and the smell and the filth and the heat, and it had not been a condition of our agreement that I would have to work on the boat. But anything to expedite the process and, besides, I might learn something.

I was lulled into a sort of a trance by the roaring of the generator and the screaming of the three grinders. Every now and then the note of the generator would rise, as a result of one of the grinders being turned off, and one of the Nikoses would appear round the side of the boat, watch my work for a bit and offer an observation on some subject not necessarily connected to the business in hand.

'Y'know Chris,' red-beard-Nikos addressed me one morning, 'it seems to me that English medieval history is very poorly documented. What is your opinion of this?'

I switched off my grinder and laid it on the ground. I looked at Nikos for a bit and he looked at me.

'Hard to say, Nikos,' I said.

He considered this for a moment, then returned to his side of the boat. I started my grinder, the generator dropped, then picked up again as the other Nikos turned his grinder off, the better to hear what his colleague had to report. They discussed my non-committal reply for a bit, then the generator took up the load again as both grinders got back to work, and we would all sink back into the working trance.

Ten minutes or so later the engine note would rise and, sure enough, the other Nikos, the handsome dark one, would appear. 'You think Shakespeare wrote all the late plays, or you reckon it was that Philip Sidney?'

In this fashion the work continued until about two o'clock, when the heat became too intense to carry on, and the Nikoses downed tools, climbed back into the *trikiklo* and went off for a siesta.

They didn't come back that first evening, and the next day they didn't turn up at all... but the day after they came and worked like lunatics without stopping, all day long. They were not what you'd call altogether reliable, but it was clear that they knew what they were doing, and little by little we got to like one another. But as the week passed, the wretched Crabber was nowhere near ready for sea. Maybe I found it hard to hide my disappointment as I waved goodbye to the Nikoses on my way to fetch Ana from the airport. I trudged off in the direction of the road. A minute later, there was red-beard-Nikos, panting by my side.

'Hey, man,' he said, dangling a primitive-looking key before my eyes. 'Take the *trikiklo*. Impress her.'

I HAD ALREADY BEEN AWAY for about a month and I was beside myself at the prospect of seeing Ana. She wore a straw hat with real cornflowers in the band and, as a consequence of a felicitous acquaintance in the airline industry, she had been plied with so much alcohol on the plane that she was almost unable to speak. Weaving in the *trikiklo* through the frenzied Athens traffic, I took her to the whorehouse where, in rather unpromising circumstances, we did what we could to become reacquainted with one another.

Later, with Annie fast asleep, I took the *trikiklo* back to the boatyard.

'So where's your girlfriend, man?' asked the Nikoses, in what I thought was a rather conspiratorial fashion.

'Er... she's sleeping. But she was certainly impressed by the *trikiklo*.'

'Well bring her down to the boat tomorrow, man. We'd sure as hell like to meet her.'

Over coffee and cake I told Ana how disappointed I was about not having the boat to take her for a spin round the islands. I had been dreaming of this ever since I had got involved with the Crabber, but now it was not to be.

'But I'd like to see your boat, anyway,' she said.

So next morning I took her down to meet the Nikoses and show her the Crabber. I thought I might have made a horrible mistake when the Nikoses turned on their Mediterranean charm and gallantry, and I felt wanting by comparison. I was just an ungainly Anglo-Saxon oaf. Ana was enchanted by the dazzling Nikoses, who had spruced themselves up to a certain limited extent for this meeting, and she also professed a certain admiration for the Crabber. All in all we spent a pleasant hour.

As we turned to leave for the shabby hotel and the grubby beach, tall-dark-Nikos beckoned me to follow him. He led us out of the boatyard and down onto the pontoons. We walked along past gleaming yachts and gin palaces, until he stopped at an unassuming little sailing boat that seemed somehow out of place amongst all the ostentatious opulence.

'There you go,' he said with a big grin, 'There's your boat. Take her away; she's all fuelled up. I guess you know how to sail, no?'

'B-but what do you mean, Nikos?' I spluttered.

'This is Nikos's boat... well, it's not exactly his, but we fixed things so you can use it. Nobody's gonna know. Go on, take Ana for a trip down the coast; Sounion is a kinda nice trip.'

I HAVE TO ADMIT THAT THE BOAT was not up to much... I mean, it was a great gesture on the part of the Nikoses, but it was disappointingly similar to Keith's wretched tub. Nonetheless, I was ecstatic at the mere thought of getting out there on that glorious sea with my girlfriend, in any kind of boat. And to Ana one boat was much like another.

So we motored out of the marina, hoisted the sail and, with me happily wielding the tiller and Ana taking instructions at the jib, we sailed away on that sunny afternoon, hugging the coast all the way down to Sounion. Towards evening we anchored in the bay about fifty yards off the beach and, with our clothes in plastic bags held high above our heads, we swam to the shore.

As night fell we wandered in the moonlight alone at the Temple of Poseidon, high on the cape of Sounion. We sat side by side on a warm rock and watched the play of the moon on the ancient white marble, and wondered at the loveliness of Greece. It put Ana in mind of poetry. She began to declaim little snatches of epic verse I'd long forgotten... if I'd ever known them at all.

'That's nice,' I said, slipping my arm round her shoulders. 'Did you just make that up?'

'It's Byron,' she replied... with just a hint of condescension in her voice. 'He sat perhaps on this very stone and I think he carved his name on one of these pillars of the temple.'

'No? Surely not... What a dastardly thing to do.'

'Indeed. And I'm pretty sure he slept here too. He was very keen on sleeping wild in classical monuments, or maybe he just liked climbing up to them to see the sunset and got stuck in the dark.'

I thought for a moment how romantic it would be to curl up together in the shelter of an ancient marble block for the night. But then I remembered how cold marble gets, and how sharp and very stony it can be, and our snug boat lulled by the calm waters seemed a much better option.

We drank wine at a taverna on the beach, and ate a sweet pink fish, alluringly arrayed upon its dish, while the foam from the wavelets lapped at our bare feet in the sand. Sated with all that succulence and not a little sodden with wine, we swam out to where the boat swung on her anchor and settled down in the balmy night air to sleep on the deck beneath the moon and stars.

Next morning we headed back, scudding on a west by northwest wind back towards the loathsome Kalamaki. It was a matter of getting the boat, which the Nikoses had clearly nicked on our behalf, back to the marina before its owner discovered its loss.

'You wanna be careful get that boat back here before two o'clock, because if not she turn into a *karpouzi*,' tall Nikos had said, rather pleased with his variation on the Cinderella theme. (A *karpouzi* is a watermelon.)

The sea was the deepest blue but for the pale white foam of the bow wave. The scents of baked rosemary and thyme and pungent, hot pine swirled in warm currents of air off the land to delight us as we passed.

ANA HAD ONLY A FEW DAYS LEFT before she had to return to Sussex. She had a business to see to. Just before I left she had begun supplying greenery to local offices to brighten their gloomy reception areas and the idea seemed to be catching on. So after little more than a week she said her fond goodbyes to the Nikoses and, loading her bags in the back, I drove her back to the airport in the trusty *trikiklo*.

For all their qualities, the Nikoses had only the shakiest grasp of the workings of time, and thus the projected week extended ever further into the distant realms of probability. Some days they came, some days they didn't, but little by little the boat started to take shape. We spent several days stuffed into the *trikiklo* cruising the business end of Piraeus looking for an engine. We found one that fit, humped it back to the Crabber and the Nikoses set about installing it. I busied myself with the less technologically demanding work of sanding down and oiling the mast and spars.

We were clearly on the final stretch now.

Then one particularly luminous morning – I remember that even in Kalamaki there was a special quality to the light reflected in the grubby scum of the harbour – Nikos handed over a crumpled message. It was from Jane, sent via Ecstaticos. She was at Spetses at last in their summer villa and there was her telephone number. I dropped my oily paintbrush and rushed to the Bar Thalassa, where as a regular customer they let me use the telephone.

'Hi Boss. How's the hips?' I asked.

'Much better now I'm here – nothing a bit of Greek sunshine and sea won't cure. Your Ecstaticos tells me the boat's nearly ready.'

'It's looking good. I don't want to be unduly optimistic... but I reckon within the week she should be done.'

'Well, that's the most marvellous news, Chris. Now tell me, would you care to come across on the hydrofoil and join us for luncheon tomorrow? I'd love you to meet our friends here and I can hand you the papers for the boat.' It seemed Captain Weare had only had photocopies.

So I took the bus along to Piraeus and hopped on a hydro-foil, one of the 'Flying Dolphins', known by the Greeks as *Flyings*. The sea was rough, so the passengers were confined, moaning and subdued, to the cabin, and all I saw of the sea and the islands was a blur of rock and water through spray-soaked windows. I buried my nose in *Zorba*. In a couple of hours, squinting against the noonday sun, I stepped onto the long concrete quay of Spetses. Cries of 'Ella, Ella' ('Here! Here!') rang out around me as the crew nonchalantly tossed ropes onto the quay. The handful of disembarking passengers shouldered their bags, some hugging waiting families or lovers; a trolley manned by a handsome brown-limbed youth picked up the parcel post. I watched as the hydrofoil eased slowly away from the dock – more cries, more snaking ropes, then I turned and followed the Spetsiots up towards the town.

My first Greek island, a richly textured little city state... It smelled of the sea, of which there was a lot, it being an island; also hot pine because what wasn't beach or olive grove or town was pine forest... and then there was fish, fresh or frying, and roasting meat. As a subtle counterpoint there was burnt petrol from the little motorbikes and vans, and from time to time an agreeable hint of drains.

Little wooden boats, blue and white, the beautiful Greek caïques, jostled one another on the swell set up by the unruly sea. Gulls cried, flapping to and fro with beakfuls of the glistening bowels of fish. Outside the *kafeneion*, fishermen sat at wooden tables dressed, like Bolsheviks, in worn shirt sleeves and frayed trousers, idly clicking their worry beads and nursing little glasses of milky ouzo and water. The town was tiny, a labyrinth of cobbled alleys clustered round the dock. The buildings blazed white in the bright sunshine, with the woodwork picked out in blue. The scale, the proportions and the colour seemed perfectly contrived to make you feel at ease. Here and there handfuls of holiday-makers ambled among the alleys, happily displaying their newly browned limbs. They smelled of the sweetest scents and suntan lotion, and they laughed and twittered in that peculiar state of abandon and gaiety that holidays bring.

The euphoria was infectious; I gave a hitch to my bag and strolled amongst the squares and alleys, my heart lightened by so much beauty and pleasure. Little by little I left behind me the hubbub and the din of the town and, following the directions that Jane had given me, climbed up through the quieter streets to the north, hugging the shade to escape the fierceness of the glaring sun. A mottled dog loped by. Somewhere a turkey gobbled. A donkey tethered in the shade of a tall eucalyptus tree brayed long and loud, enough to break your heart.

'The reason a donkey makes that heart-rending noise', I reflected, thinking of country lore, 'is because the donkey has seen the devil.'

To Spiti Joyce – The Joyce House – Jane had told me, could be located by means of a tall eucalyptus with a donkey teth-ered to it. I crossed a shadeless stretch of waste ground and pulled the bell set in a high white wall. I waited in the shade of an overhanging oleander; the hot air thick with the sweet scent of jasmine and the pleasant cat-piss smell of fig.

A fumbling on the far side of the door, and there was Bob. 'Well, if it isn't our new skipper... Delighted to see you, Chris. Come and join us; we have a few friends over for luncheon.'

I dumped my bag on the cobbles of the patio, mussed up my hair a little with my hands and dusted myself down, then followed Bob through into the cool of the house and out onto the terrace. Here, beneath the dappled shade of a spreading fig, was set the table, a simple calico cloth and some fresh flowers, some glimmering glasses with cool white wine. By this time I was steeped in euphoria; the contrast between the grimness of Kalamaki and this lovely Mediterranean island was almost too much to take in.

'Chris, what perfect timing,' called Jane from her seat at the head of the table. She seemed not a jot altered by her hospital ordeal. 'I shall not rise to greet you, dear boy,' she continued beckoning me forward, 'as my wretched new titanium bones dictate that I remain seated, but help yourself to a glass of wine and come and give an account of yourself. These are our good friends.'

There were not many friends: an elderly Greek couple, expensively dressed and coiffed and just a shade reserved; I shook their hands. Next to them sat a much younger woman, slim with thick dark hair twisted into a knot at the nape of her neck. She looked up at me, her brown eyes alight with amused intelligence.

And this', enunciated Jane, 'is Florica.'

Well, I liked the look of Florica. She had a casual grace that immediately put you at your ease and a dazzling smile. I kissed her on each cheek and sat down rather presumptuously beside her. A hint of lemon blossom wafted across as she turned to ask me how the fiasco with the boat was going. Her voice was low, her accent cosmopolitan.

Jane surveyed us with the satisfied expression of a benign aunt. 'Let's wait for Tim, my dears; then we can eat lunch and Chris can tell us about the unfortunate Crabber,' she said. Then added, 'I think you'll hit it off with Tim. He's English, you know, and a writer and can turn his hand to absolutely anything. He's so wonderfully clever.'

As if on cue the bell jangled.

A tall, tanned man stepped into the courtyard and greeted Jane and Bob with unaffected warmth; the Greeks he greeted politely in Greek. Then, pulling up a chair next to Florica, he extended a hand, almost as calloused as my own. 'I was doing a little carpentry on the house,' he explained to the guests, 'and I completely lost track of time; do forgive me if I've kept you waiting.'

You could easily forgive Tim. He had a keen sympathy and a look of such absorbed interest in whatever you happened to be saying that stories just spilled out. Soon I was recounting the desperate goings on at Kalamaki Marina, the perfidy of Captain Bob, and the surprising erudition of the Nikoses. All of which Tim translated fluently for the Greeks while I watched, smiling at his gently incredulous tone and the habitual way that he blinked whenever he was about to voice a new thought. It was obvious that he and Florica were lovers, and I decided to myself that a friendship with this delightful couple would put the finishing touches to my idyllic summer.

The lunch of course helped. There were bright salads of divinely sweet tomatoes, with Kalamata olives and chunks of fresh feta cheese; a bowl of taramasalata – creamed roes and garlic and lemon and heaven knows what else was in it; and tzatziki too, with rich yoghurt, salt and the crispest cucumber. There were tin jugs of cold retsina with condensation dribbling down the outside, for those who fancied that pungent resinous taste. For the more delicate palates a big bottle of cool Cambas white wine. Later came a dish of delicately poached *barbounia* – red mullet – with some courgettes and aubergines done with parsley to perfection.

It seemed to me at that moment as if everything was in harmony: the food, the colours, the people, the hot sun, the view of the little harbour and the blue sea below... as if I'd passed through a portal into a different, more congenial dimension.

Tim was a walker and a climber and lover of the mountains, and was writing a book about the mountains of Greece. I dearly wanted to go to the mountains, too. One thing that we both emphatically agreed upon was that we always – and neither of us ever made an exception to this rule – travelled alone. So when Tim told me that he was planning to go for a ten-day journey into the Pindus, up near the Macedonian border, I thought about it for a bit, and then said, 'Can I come along too?'

He looked at me in surprise, and hesitated just a moment before saying, 'Yes, why not? That would be very nice.'

'And come to think of it,' I continued pensively, 'I'm going to need somebody to help me bring the boat down from Kalamaki to Spetses. Are you a sailor?'

Now, to a seasoned nautical man, the business of sailing a Cornish Crabber single-handed down the Saronic Gulf in the summer would offer little difficulty... but you never know, and besides it would be nice to have some company.

'Never been on a sailing boat in my life,' he replied, blinking hard, 'but I'd be very happy to give it a go.'

IN PRAISE OF A BUCKET

TIM HAD A GOOD IDEA TO START OFF WITH, suggesting that we took the ferry, rather than the hydrofoil, back to Athens, in order to stand on deck and get a good look at the route that we would be taking with the Crabber, when and if it were ever ready. We duly took note of every islet and peninsula along the way – and noted, too, that one island looks much like another from the sea. But it was a fairly straightforward route: sail close to the shore and keep the land on your left – or your right, that would be, coming from Athens.

Once at Piraeus we took the bus along to Kalamaki Marina. It was a Monday and by the time we got to the yard it was long into the searing heat of siesta time, a time when the Nikoses would never deign to work. But there was the *trikiklo*, and as we approached the Crabber we heard the sound of banging – the universal concomitant of men and work – coming from deep in the bowels of the boat. And then red-beard-Nikos, caked in engine grease and soaked in sweat, a truly disgusting sight, clambered out of the hole where the engine lived, and announced: 'That's it, man. Noo engine in. All we need now is get the boat rigged. I reckon we get it done tonight, you fill up some gas and tomorrow morning you sail away to Spetses.'

I figured that the way to get an undertaking like this on the move was to throw some cold beer at it, so I took the *trikiklo* to town and bought a couple of crates.

When I got back, the frenetic pace of the work had subsided a little, as the Nikoses and Tim were squatting in the dust in the shade of the boat, deep in discussion of the anti-fascist poetry of Seferis and Gatsos. At least, that's what Tim said. They were all talking Greek, Tim with an easy fluency that made the Nikoses seem even better company in their native language. I felt the smallest bit left out.

'Right,' I shouted. 'Enough with the literary seminars, let's get this boat rigged.'

Little by little, by judicious application of warming beer and the sharp side of my tongue, I managed to get them moving. By the cool of the evening we were ready to raise the mast. We hauled it up, gleaming with a dozen coats of oil, tightened all the ropes that held it in place and then fitted the boom. At last the Crabber started to look like a sailing boat. I climbed off her time after time just to go and stand at a distance and admire the sight. Night fell and at last she was all set to go. The plan was that the Nikoses would make the arrangements with the harbour crane to put her in the water first thing in the morning; Tim and I would gather the necessary provisions, and we would set off as early as possible. I reckoned that, all being well, the journey to Spetses, fifty-seven nautical miles away, ought to take us about twelve hours.

Of course, next morning the Nikoses failed to show up. I was in a state of excitement verging upon hysteria and Tim got so fed up with me moaning on about the Nikoses – where were the buggers? – that he marched off and sorted out the harbour crane himself. It took an hour; these things are best done at a steady pace... one small slip with a harbour crane and that's the end of your boat. But finally there was the Crabber – a boat really ought to have a name, but the Crabber was always known as 'the Crabber' – in her proper element, floating in the water.

Tim excelled himself further by fixing the paperwork with the harbour authorities; we loaded the water, figs, dates, olives and bread, our iron rations (in case things cut up really rough), filled the tank with diesel... and cast off.

Bub... bub... bub, bub, bubbububbubbub went the engine, a big inboard diesel with a deep pleasing throb. I let Tim take the tiller while I flaked down the warps – this seemed no time to give a lesson in what a warp was and how to flake it – and we throbbed slowly along between the pontoons, nosing through the slicks of oil and rafts of floating rubbish. Tim pushed the tiller across and we edged between the breakwaters and at long last out into the mighty rolling blue sea.

As I looked back, I could just make out a *trikiklo* bouncing along the harbour mole. It pulled up at the end and disgorged the Nikoses, who jumped up and down, and waved encouragingly for a bit. We waved back in a more restrained, Anglo-Saxon manner before returning to the business of setting sail. 'Head into the wind and we'll get the sails up and we can turn that horrible engine off.' I shouted.

Now with most people, if you were to tell them to head into wind, they wouldn't have a clue what you were talking about, but Tim was a natural. I busied myself with the mess of tangled ropes and pulleys on the foredeck, and within twenty minutes or so had the sails all hoisted. I turned the engine off and we abandoned ourselves to the sounds of the sea and the gentle breeze coming out of the north.

ON A CLEAR DAY – and this was the clearest of days – you can see the island of Aegina from the harbour mouth at Kalamaki. It appears as a slightly darker grey blue than the grey blue of the mountains on the mainland behind, and the nearer you approach, the more it detaches itself, until finally it appears as a living island with its forest of pines and its cliffs and coves and villages. I figured that because it was our first time out, it might be better to hop from island to island on the way down, following the ferry route, rather than launch ourselves out into the open sea.

The little wind we had was just about right to get us to Aegina, so I pulled the tiller over, let out the main until it blossomed with wind, then cleated the sheet home. Tim adjusted the jib and the staysail until they were smooth like a well-ironed sheet and full of the breeze, and the little boat bounded away across the blue sparkling water, shattering the wavelets into trails of pale foam. Oh lord, were there words to convey the simple joy of feeling the pull of the tiller on a sailing boat scudding across the bright blue sea in the sunshine? I laughed and I laughed and my eyes filled with tears, partly from the breeze and the salt-laden spray, but partly, if the truth be told, from sheer ecstasy.

Little by little the port suburbs of Athens dropped away astern, the sea became deeper and bluer... and then the wind dropped. The cat's-paw wavelets on the surface disappeared and the sea turned glassy. The Crabber stopped her headlong motion.

You always think of the Ancient Mariner at times like these, dragging around the carcass of the albatross, decrying the terrible stillness and silence of the sea. But in reality it's not silent at all. With the gentle rocking of the boat and not a breath to keep the tension, the heavy boom swung inboard and then out with a crash that made the whole boat shudder. It did this about every twenty seconds and within ten minutes our nerves were utterly frazzled.

'Isn't there anything we can do to stop that horrible crashing?' asked Tim.

'Well, as a matter of fact there is, but it would impede our progress.'

'We're not exactly making a lot of progress anyway, are we? What can we do?'

'Well, we could tie a bucket to the end of the boom and throw it in the water. The drag would restrain the boom from banging... but it's a hideously unseamanlike solution. And we haven't actually brought a bucket with us.'

'But we have to do something. We can't just sit here like this; we'll go bonkers.'

'Heavens, man – we've only been becalmed for fifteen minutes.'

'Perhaps,' agreed Tim. 'But the problem with the Mediterranean is that in summer the calms are almost constant. The Ancients didn't do very much sailing at all, you know; they rowed everywhere. But they didn't have the internal combustion engine then, of course,' he added as an afterthought. Then blinked.

'Of course,' I echoed thoughtfully, wondering what he was driving at.

'We have, though.'

'We have what?' I asked, absently.

'Internal combustion engines... We have an internal combustion engine right here on this boat.'

'Aah...'

'So why don't we start it up?'

I had suspected all along that this was what Tim wanted: he wanted to forget sailing and use the engine.

'Well, it's smelly and noisy, and it makes the whole thing rather disagreeable, don't you think?'

'But surely it can't be more disagreeable than sitting here becalmed with that boom banging the hell out of the poor boat. And besides, we're supposed to get to Spetses today... At this rate we're not even going to make it to Aegina.'

There was something in what Tim had to say. I held my ground a little longer... then I started up the engine.

WE PULLED THE SAILS IN TIGHT and set course for the northern tip of Aegina. With our forward speed an apparent wind sprang up and cooled us down; the warm sunshine had become a searing furnace while we were becalmed. The Crabber churned on across the glassy waters towards Aegina, and the progress cheered us up. The engine didn't sound too bad, a pleasant chugging coming from somewhere deep down inside the boat. We ate some figs and had a sip of water. It wouldn't do to get dehydrated.

'What's that smell?' asked Tim.

'What smell?'

'There's a sort of a hot smell.'

'That'll be the engine, I suppose.'

'But it didn't smell like that before.'

'No, that's because we had it turned off.'

'No, but I mean since we've had it running.'

'Engines always smell like that when they're running – it's because they get hot. And this one is new, so probably all the paint is burning off it. It's what always happens.' I rabbited on, not altogether convinced by my own sophistry.

Then a plume of smoke appeared from under the lid of the engine cover.

'Jesus, the goddamn boat's on fire!' Tim cried.

'Nonsense, man. It's just a bit of hot paint. I'll take the cover off it.'

I shipped the tiller out of the way and bent down to lift the heavy wooden cover off the engine box. It was hard to budge – and a little hot – and when I finally shifted it it came away with a great jerk. A thick cloud of black smoke burst upon us and, with the sudden hit of oxygen from the violently lifted lid, the whole damn thing burst into flames.

'Fuck! You're right. We're on fire. Get some water, quick!'

'How?'

'From the sea, of course! Get some water out of the sea with a bucket!'

'But we haven't got a fucking bucket! We haven't got anything for chrissakes!'

The essence of being a good seaman is to keep your head when things go wrong, as in their inimitable way they inevitably will, and to be able to improvise. How to put out a fire at sea without a bucket... hmm.

'I know,' said Tim, 'we can take our shirts off and dip them in the sea and wring them out over the engine.'

No sooner said than done. We dipped and scooped and wrung for all we were worth. And by this method we soon doused the flames, mainly because they had already consumed the piece of wood they were interested in – a small section of bulkhead that was too close to the really hot bit of the engine.

We sat back and wiped the sweat from our eyes. There was a horrible sizzling, a smell of oily smoke and steam.

'There must be something not quite right,' I observed. 'It's not supposed to do that.'

Tim refrained from making any comment, for which I was grateful. He blinked down at his sodden shirt.

'I think it's a mistake to put to sea without a bucket,' he suggested. 'I suppose we'll have to return to Kalamaki and see about getting it fixed.'

'Not bloody likely,' I cried. 'I'd sooner die than go back to that hellhole. We're heading to Aegina.'

This ill-considered utterance produced a silence between us. Neither of us quite knew how to put what we were thinking. Eventually Tim spoke. 'And how', he said, 'would we get to Aegina if, say, we were to want to go there?'

'Well we'd have to sail, wouldn't we?'

I was very conscious of being the skipper here, and it was my clear duty not to spread panic amongst the rather volatile crew. I would play the nastiness of our situation down. Things were, after all, about as bad as things could get. Here we were, out in the middle of the ocean, midway between Kalamaki and Aegina, in a boat that would at the least provocation, so it seemed, burst into flames. There was not a breath of wind to take us anywhere and, perhaps worst of all, we had no bucket. On the positive side we had some figs and dates and olives and a couple of bottles of drinking water.

'But there isn't any wind,' said Tim with irritating predictability. 'Here we are out in the middle of the sodding ocean...'

'It's not an ocean,' I interrupted testily. 'It's a sea. We are, if I'm not mistaken, in the Aegean.'

'Now, let's face it, Chris, it doesn't make a whole lot of difference to our plight whether it's an ocean or a sea, does it?'

WHICHEVER WAY WE LOOKED AT IT, our situation was grim. If we'd had a radio or some such thing, we could have radioed for help... but, as I've already been at pains to point out, we didn't even have a sodding bucket. I could see that Tim was wondering about the wisdom of having invited a person such as me to share his journey to the mountains.

The Crabber lifted and fell almost imperceptibly on the gentle swell. The boom swung regularly to and fro, each time with a sickening crash. The sun poured down upon our unprotected heads. It was far from pleasant. A resolution had to be made, in order to move us out of the disagreeable state of affairs in which we found ourselves and into the next one, whatever that might prove to be.

We resolved to keep the sails trimmed in order to take advantage of even the slightest passing zephyr. We had already observed, by dint of spitting into the sea and watching the boat's movement in relation to the bubbles thus produced, that although we appeared to be standing stock-still we were in fact heading in an unspectacular fashion towards Aegina. There was some considerable distance left to cover, about six nautical miles I reckoned, but the likelihood was that as the long day drew towards evening a breeze might spring up and, all being well, we could be in the harbour by nightfall.

We amused ourselves for a time by studying the engine and its mountings, to see if we could discover the cause of the fire. Neither Tim nor I, though, are of a mechanical turn of mind, and so the exercise consisted in not much more than staring into the engine hold in bovine fashion and shaking our heads in disbelief.

'We could', suggested Tim, 'try running the engine again, for a short time, and see what happens.'

'It's a bit of a risk,' I said. 'If the boat catches fire properly, we're doomed.'

Oddly enough fire at sea is one of the worst of the mariner's fears; it's the canvas and the wood and the usually strong wind to fan the flames, the presence of the three elements, air, fire and water... and the absence of the fourth, the blessed unyielding earth, that make it such a nightmare.

But it was worth a try so, nervously, we started the engine again. It seemed to run fine, so, leaving the cover off, we slipped it into gear. Again the blessed cooling breeze, the churning of the wake astern. I spat in the sea. The filmy bubbles vanished behind us in seconds.

'There's that smell again,' said Tim.

I peered into the hold. Sure enough the curl of blue smoke, the woodwork glowing like hot coals. I pulled the stop knob and the silence reasserted itself. It had been no more than five minutes, but five minutes at five knots, and the little bit of freewheeling at the end, take you the best part of half a mile. Aegina was definitely a lot nearer than Kalamaki now. We felt heartened a little by this.

So now we figured that we could use the engine in brief bursts in an emergency, but any more than five minutes would have the Crabber engulfed in flames. It was going to be a long, long afternoon.

I decided to teach Tim some knots to while away the time. We may not have had a bucket, but the Crabber was well supplied with bits of old rope. Rather pleased with my own recently gleaned knowledge and love of knots, I showed him the amazing bowline and its interesting qualities and uses; then we did the clove hitch, the reef knot and the granny, all of which he knew already. Then on to the more complicated rolling hitch, the Fisherman's hitch, the sheepshank, the sheet bend, the Sailors' knot and the beautiful Turk's Head. This activity occupied us for more than an hour, and it was an hour in which, apart from the study of the knots and its attendant self-improvement, we made not the slightest bit of progress. We had given up spitting into the sea, partly in order to conserve bodily liquids, but partly too because neither of us felt it was quite the right thing to do. In our precarious situation the last thing we wanted to do was give offence to, say, Neptune, or Doris and her sisters. It was pretty obvious we were not getting anywhere, anyway.

Next we told stories, mostly of a salacious and mildly humorous type, but of this we soon tired. Finally Tim started to tell me about Greek history. He did this so well that I was absolutely captivated and time seemed to pass in a completely different way. Almost before I knew it, the sun had dipped behind the mountains and we were in blessed shade.

Tim was sitting with his back against the mast, while I lay slumped in the cockpit idly waggling the tiller. We had moved a long way back through history, and Tim was onto the War of Independence: '...and then there was Athanasios Diakos – the Turks broke every bone in his body with hammers, before impaling him...' when all of a sudden the boat heeled hard over.

'The wind, the wind,' we cried, as we let out the sails and sheeted them home, and the Crabber leaped and scudded eagerly towards the west. In less than an hour we were rounding the point at the northern tip of the island. Night was falling and the lights of the little town were just coming on.

We switched direction without mishap and with the wind now coming over our port quarter we eased down the west side of the island.

THIS WAS WHERE OUR NEXT PROBLEM APPEARED. In Greece the convention is to moor your boat stern to; that is, with the back of the boat against the quay and the bow facing outwards, kept in check by the anchor. In order to achieve this there is a complex manoeuvre which involves sailing past the slot where you have decided to moor your boat, then backing in, dropping the anchor on the way. You let the anchor line run as you move carefully backward, your fenders down to cushion the inevitable crunching of the neighbouring boats. At the last moment, just as you are about to crash into the dock, you kill the engine, snag the anchor line and leap off onto the shore with your mooring warps to make them fast. This is all done in one swift movement. Unfortunately, I had never performed the manoeuvre before and my engine was, to say the least, unreliable.

I was understandably a little nervous as we rounded up outside the dock and dropped the sails. I started the engine, and we moved slowly backwards towards the berth we had chosen.

'Drop anchor,' I cried in a nautical fashion, and Tim dropped the anchor, letting the line run out through the fairlead.

'Make fast to the bitts!' and Tim, without a moment's hesitation, made fast to the bitts, as I had briefed him to do. I switched off the engine and leaped onto the shore, at the same moment as the Crabber pulled up just half a yard short of the dock. I took a turn round a bollard with the mooring warps and jumped back on board to cleat them off.

I looked at Tim and Tim looked back at me. Nothing had gone wrong; the whole daunting manoeuvre had gone off without mishap. It was almost too much to take on board. Later we sat in a taverna by the dock drinking retsina, rather a lot of it, and discussing our next move. If we had had half a brain between us we would have gone to a boatyard on Aegina and got the boat fixed there and then. But I felt that we had already started our journey. Spetses was not so very far away now, and I was keen to get the boat down to its home. Also a certain mood of unfounded optimism had taken hold as a result of the success of the docking and the pleasant hour of sailing we had enjoyed on the wings of the evening breeze. In short, we had completely forgotten how awful the previous day had been.

We decided to leave for Spetses the next morning, engine or no engine. But we did take the precaution of buying a big red plastic bucket.

BRIMMING WITH CONFIDENCE in our new-found powers of seamanship, we left the dock without the engine, under sail. This was a matter of casting off the mooring lines, pushing off and heaving on the anchor line to get a bit of speed up, then raising the staysail, sheeting it hard in so the breeze carried the bow round... then finally up with all the sails and off and away to the south. The whole manoeuvre unfolded flawlessly, seemingly without effort.

As we sailed slowly along the west coast of the island the breeze began to freshen and veered a little until it was blowing strongly from the northeast. Tim was on the tiller and I was on the foredeck fooling around with the sails. We shot out from the end of the island and turned a little to the east in order to go round the outside of Poros instead of navigating the narrow channel between the island and the mainland.

There were about twelve miles from the southern tip of Aegina to Hydra, where we would be bearing west for the final run home to Spetses. It took us not much more than a couple of hours, about as fast as a little boat like this could go. Tim, who was learning fast how to feel the wind with a delicate touch of the tiller, how to keep the sails filled and working to drive us forward, was a natural. And I could tell that he was ecstatic about this new experience. As was I; our whole beings were suffused with the sheer joy of wind and water and sunshine, and the beauty of our little craft. For this, too, is a big part of the pleasure, the way a boat moves in the water, whether she be gliding across the still waters of a sheltered bay or – in that school anthology poem of Masefield's – 'butting through the Channel in the mad March days'.

No wonder people get emotional about their boats. Because boats – or, at any rate, old wooden boats – have their personalities, their foibles, their weaknesses and their beauty. The wind sings in the rigging; the hull creaks and groans as the stays take the strain of the wind in the sails; then there's the clanking and rattle of the winches, of the blocks and tackles, of the hoists and lifts and purchases, the jolly rollicking of the parrel balls as they roll up and down the mast. There's the smells too, the wood and the oil, the unforgettable smell of tarred twine and Stockholm tar; there'll always be an undertone of fish, too, and the huge smell of the sea.

And the beauty, the incomparable beauty, of sailing boats is a thing that has settled deep in my heart and it's hard to get rid of it. Of all the beautiful things that mankind by his creative genius and his ability to co-operate has created, it's the tea clipper, racing home from China under full press of sail, that is the absolute zenith for me. There are those who would cite aircraft and rocket ships or buildings... and

I concede the beauty of, say, Concorde, even the space shuttle, and the Parthenon... but still, number one on my list is the Cutty Sark.

And the fact that there is so much lore and literature about boats is because sailing goes back to the dawn of history; it goes deep into the genes of our island races, and if one is not a lover of poetry and literature, then there are few better ways to become one than to spend time sailing in small boats.

We raced on, hour after hour across the wine-dark sea... not really like wine at all, but a deep, deep blue that gave the impression of unimaginable depth. The lovely treeless island of Hydra appeared on our bow, pale and stark and rising sheer in grey and red cliffs from the waters. We stuffed ourselves with bread and olives and figs and watched the ferries and fishing boats busying themselves around the mouth of the tiny harbour.

Finally we cut between the end of Hydra and the bare uninhabited rock of Trikiri, and there, barely five miles off, lay Spetses. The wind dropped a little and there was only the lightest of swells on the sea as we pulled away again into the open water.

Tim and I were getting cocky; we had been sailing fast and easy all day long and now our bourn was in sight. We wanted a little more of a challenge.

'Right,' I said. 'Let's do a man-overboard drill. Test ourselves a little.'

'What would that involve?' asked Tim.

'Well, it's a thing you do when you learn to sail, one of the most important of all, really. You throw a buoy overboard and then do the appropriate manoeuvre to pick it up, as if it were a real person.'

'Sounds like fun. What shall we throw overboard? I know: the bucket.'

'Over my dead body; the bucket is the most important thing on the boat. I know, you jump overboard and I'll do the stuff and pick you up.'

'OK,' said Tim. 'I could do with a swim.' And before I could utter another word, he was gone, a neat dive deep down beneath the surface. A few seconds later he was up and spluttering. 'Jesus, man, it's just beautiful. Come on in.'

'I don't think that would be a very good idea. Just hang on in there and I'LL SEE IF I CAN REMEMBER HOW TO DO THIS.' I had to shout the last few words because we were already quite a way apart.

Now, what you are supposed to do is the following: you harden your sheets and work upwind of your man, tack, then go downwind of your man, then harden up, and just as you come up to windward of your man you let fly your sheets and come, all being well, to a stop with your man just beneath your lee bow.

I muttered the formula uneasily to myself as I pushed the tiller over, and, keeping an eye on the head bobbing about among the distant waves, cleated in the sheets as we came close to the wind. I ducked as the boom flew across, and, sheeting in the headsails on the other side, I lost sight momentarily of my man.

'Now where's that man?... TI-I-I-M,' I cried.

'OVER HERE,' he yelled. I saw him splashing.

'OK, here we come.'

The last bit was to head a little downwind of him, then come back up on the wind... at least I was heading towards him now. Things were looking up. Finally there he was, dead on the bow – metaphorically speaking. I turned upwind some more so that he slipped along the lee side, and then I let the sheets fly.

'There,' I said. 'How about that, then? Piece of cake.'

There wasn't very much wind now, so the operation was not too difficult, but even so it was amazing how quickly we had moved apart. Tim hauled himself with impressive agility back into the boat.

'Right,' I said. 'Your go now. Let's see how you make out.'

'Oh, I'm not so sure,' he demurred. 'I don't think I'm ready for this yet...'

'Nonsense, man. You'll have no trouble at all.'

And I explained to him clearly and succinctly the moves of the drill.

'So now imagine you're sailing along just like this,' I said, handing Tim the tiller, 'and all of a sudden your man falls overboard... thus...' Saying which I dived off the back as deep as I could go. I swam down and down, then twisted to come up again. I saw the tiny distant light of the sun, eclipsed by the bluest blueness that the mind could imagine. So much beauty... Then I shot out into a burst of sunlit spray. I spluttered and caught my breath.

Where was the Crabber? I looked all around. Christ, it was halfway to Spetses! I could see Tim buggering about ineffectually with the tiller and the sheets.

'WHAT THE HELL WAS I SUPPOSED TO DO NEXT?' he shouted.

'HARDEN YOUR SHEETS AND TURN INTO WIND.'

He flapped about a bit and then headed off upwind.

Perhaps at this point I should say that we were lunatics enough to do this without wearing lifejackets.

'OK. NOW WHAT?'

'NOW TACK, TURN RIGHT, SLACKEN OFF YOUR SHEETS AND HEAD OFF OVER THERE UNTIL I SAY SO.'

The Crabber came through the wind and rocketed off downwind of me. I was treading water and trying hard not to think of all the horrible denizens of the deep with intentions inimical to my well-being.

'RIGHT, NOW TURN LEFT, SHEET IN YOUR SAILS AND HEAD FOR TRIKIRI. ON THE WAY YOU OUGHT TO PASS ME.'

It all took a long time, and I did have some uneasy moments, but I live to tell the tale.

BY THE TIME WE HAD FINISHED FOOLING AROUND in the water, the wind had dropped to the merest breath, but the island was barely a couple of miles off now. We could see the little lighthouse on the rocks at the mouth of the harbour.

'You know there'll be a party on the dock to welcome our arrival, don't you?' said Tim.

'I doubt it. Nobody knows exactly when we're going to arrive... least of all us,' I added glumly as I looked up at the sagging sails.

'Oh, they'll know alright; someone will have spotted us as soon as we sailed out from behind Hydra.'

'It seems a little unlikely,' I protested.

'Not a bit,' countered Tim. 'We're the only boat round here with red sails – you can see us coming a mile off – and Jane and her friends spend half their day sitting on their terraces, drinking gin and watching the sea. Not to mention the fact that it's the Bouboulina festival.'

'And just what exactly is Bouboulina?'

'Bouboulina', explained Tim, 'was a Spetsiot admiral during the War of Independence – a female admiral, to be exact. And, among her many exploits, she put to rout the Ottoman navy in Spetses harbour – which is what the whole shindig commemorates.'

'How did she set about that? I asked, getting interested now.

'Fireships,' said Tim. 'She set fire to a number of her ships and sailed them into the midst of the tightly packed Ottoman fleet. Burned the lot to a frazzle.' He looked at me meaningfully to see if the full impact of Bouboulina's deeds was getting through. 'So you can take it from me, most of the island will be down at the port, with the priests and dignitaries doing their stuff... so we'd better not cock up our arrival, had we?'

'Oh, I think we've got pretty competent now,' I said, giving a little more slack to the staysail. 'But we could be hours yet if this wind doesn't pick up. I wonder if we ought to give the engine another try.'

'Go on, then – we're almost home anyway. Maybe the thing that was making it get so hot has loosened up. We can always turn it off if things start to cut up rough.'

So I turned the key and a little nervously pushed the starter. The engine burst into life and once again we surged on towards Spetses and the waiting welcome committee.

It held out well this time; I was running it slowly, just above the idle, to keep it as cool as possible, because I knew we would need it for the final docking manoeuvre and, as my crew had so succinctly pointed out, we didn't want to make a cock-up of it.

We puttered slowly around the point and turned in towards the harbour. Tim was right: there on the dock was Jane, transported in what looked like a home-made litter. She sat in this contrivance and held court amongst the score or so of friends who surrounded her, in their summer glad rags, and she like some queen of ancient times about to bless the waves. But that wasn't the half of it. As Tim had suggested, the whole damn island was down there too, whooping it up on the dock. There were rockets and a band and buckets of booze and Bouboulina herself was there, magnificent in effigy, a great papier-mâché lady admiral, glowering censoriously out across the water.

'We'd better make this look good,' I said. 'Or we're going to look prize arse'oles. There's enough of a breeze now to sail in... Let's do it.'

I cut the engine and brought the Crabber round. Tim trimmed the sails and she heeled gently and started her final run into the harbour. The wind direction wasn't quite right, but it would just about do. We were going to end up just a little further away from the dock than I would have liked, but no matter.

As soon as we came into view we heard loud cheers from Jane's contingent – we must have cut a fine dash with all the red sails up and pulling – followed by a frenzied toasting and waving of scarves and kerchiefs. We smiled and waved to the happy crowd.

At the last moment I rounded up and started the engine, just letting it tick over for when we needed it. We dropped the sails and bundled them up neatly in a tight harbour stow.

'Better make this a bit snappy,' observed Tim. 'She's starting to smoke.'

'Jee-zus, you're right.' She wasn't just starting to smoke; we'd been too busy with the sails to notice, but there were clouds of smoke belching from the engine hold now. There was the faintest sense of consternation coming off the land, murmurs of concern, questions asked... Was this perhaps some part of the Bouboulina festivities?

We drifted further away from the mooring, not waving and smiling now, but panicking just a bit as we tried to retrieve something of the dignity of the occasion. Tim was on the foredeck, ready to do his stuff with the anchor. I jammed the engine into reverse and hit the throttle by mistake. The engine howled and promptly burst into flames. The boat rocketed backwards towards the dock, belching smoke and flame. A Greek fire ship in reverse. The Bouboulina revellers on the dock scattered like ninepins – all except newly hipped Jane, enthroned amongst the greenery and flowers of the makeshift litter.

'Anchor aweigh.'

'What?'

'DROPANCHORFORCHRISSAKES!! NOW!'

Tim dropped the anchor as we hurtled back. I hit the gear lever. Damn thing jammed. Engulfed now in the fire and smoke, I jabbed and tugged for all I was worth at the lever.

'SNAGOFFTHEANCHORLINENOW!' I yelled above the foul din... just as a moment later with a satisfying crunch the Crabber crashed at speed into the stone dock.

Jane rose a little unsteadily from her litter, leaning on her stick, and cried, '*Sto kalo*, all to the good, dear Chris. Welcome. I am overjoyed to see you and the Crabber safe and sound.'

IF JANE WAS A LITTLE DISAPPOINTED by the spectacular mode of our arrival, she was kind enough not to show it. Loyalty was one of her finer qualities, and I think she had decided that after all my tribulations in Kalamaki I deserved a break.

Florica, who was also there on the dock, gave us a touching account of Jane's spirited defence of her new skipper, to the less-than-impressed party of guests. Florica herself, though, had some searching questions of her own to ask us, such as why, when we knew the engine was faulty, hadn't we stayed on at Aegina and arranged for it to be repaired? It was a suggestion that left us both, and especially the more responsible Tim, feeling somewhat sheepish. He redeemed himself by introducing me to the island's best mechanic, who had the engine fixed by the end of the week.

Sadly, neither Tim and Florica could stay much longer than that. They had work to return to in Athens and London and were soon boarding the hydrofoil themselves. We parted with plans to meet up in London and, unusually for a holiday friendship, we each of us knew that we would. And so my summer job finally began.

As summer jobs go – indeed, jobs of any kind – this was a pretty good one. My duties were simply to keep the boat and myself in readiness to take Jane and her friends out on the water at any time of night or day.

Occasionally we would take the boat across the straits to a waterfront taverna on the mainland, setting out from the simple wooden jetty close to Jane and Bob's house. We would leave in the cool of the evening, just as the sun, draine d of its noonday ferocity, sank towards the blue hills of the Peloponnese. This was a lovely hour to go sailing, on the gentlest of evening breezes and the sea almost shimmering. For a couple of hours we would sail lazily northward, trailing fingers and toes in the calm water till we dropped the sails and drifted deftly alongside the wooden tables at the quayside where we were to meet some of Jane and Bob's friends for dinner.

Dinner would go on for hours and I would sit with the boat tied, like an obedient dog, to my chair leg. The little harbour teemed with fish and there were candles in jam jars on the tables, the scent of jasmine and honeysuckle complemented by dishes of fried squid with the lightest coating of batter glistening with droplets of freshly squeezed lemon. Later, as the pale moon rose over the dark bulk of Trikiri, we would motor back to the island, shattering into bright shards the moonlight that lay on the still water. Jane would take the tiller and dream perhaps of her girlhood down in the Deep South, of the days when she could run fast and easy and dance all night. Bob would smoke and quietly tell stories that Jane must have heard a hundred times before, yet managed to greet with a look of amused attention. And me, I sat leaning against the mast in the dark, captivated by it all.

At other times we might load the boat with food and wine and sail round the island to some quiet bay for a picnic beneath the pines on the beach, and there we would loll till late in the afternoon, in the glorious scented shade of warm Mediterranean pine. Or we might sail on to the house of one of their friends who had a waterside home with its own jetty and there take a lingering lunch through the long hot hours of the afternoon. Usually I would be invited too, but on the odd occasion when the hosts were especially superior people, I would stay on the boat, munch sandwiches and read some poetry books that Tim had left me – the very Seferis and Gatsos recommended by the Nikoses. And I'd swim, of course. Whenever the heat or tiredness overtook me, I'd simply plunge into the water and circle the boat for a while.

There were times, too, on those fiercely hot late summer days when there was just nowhere to get cool on the land. On those days we would take the Crabber out and sail to and fro, luxuriating in the blessed coolness of the wind on the water. I figured from the paths of conversation that this would probably be Jane's last year with the Crabber, and it was up to me to do what I could to help make it a good one.

If the seas were too rough, we'd stay at home, lounge about, read, or take long siestas. The deal had been that I would live on the boat, which was fine for the odd night, but a bit of an ordeal for much longer. Fortunately, though, my employers insisted that I take a spare room in their villa. The very essence of minimalism it was, with a red tiled floor, a bed and a chair with a mosquito coil smoking through the night. I would breakfast alone with a book, in the shade of a fig tree, on toast and butter and honey and yoghurt, washed down with 'mountain tea'; lunch and dinner we would take together on the terrace.

As late summer moved into autumn the high winds and stormy seas confined us more and more to the land. The pinewoods that crowned the hill above the town burst forth with a carpet of beautiful little Mediterranean cyclamen. At night there was the smell of woodsmoke, and the occasional squall of rain would come tearing across the Saronic Gulf and lash the island for an hour or so. All the summer visitors had gone and we began to make preparations to close the house up for the winter. Finally came the morning on which I helped carry Bob and Jane's baggage down to the town.

I laid their bags on the dock, amongst the usual milling crowd of Spetsiots who waited, with their trolleys and heaps of mysterious boxes and parcels tied with string, for the mid-morning hydrofoil.

'My dear,' said Jane, as the craft came into view, 'I can't pretend to know what next year will bring. At our age we're happy just to enjoy the present. But as long as we keep my lovely Crabber you must come and sail her. There'll always be a place for you here.'

I hugged her warmly.

'Goodbye, skipper,' said Bob, extending his hand. 'It has been a great pleasure. Please come and visit with us in London.'

I saw them climb on board, and stood on the dock and waved until I could see them no more. Then I turned and walked along the jetty to the town, where I had a coffee and a honey bun, before strolling along to the boatyard to make arrangements for taking the Crabber out of the water.

PART THREE

Cutting Up Rough

VINLAND VOYAGE

IN THE WINTER, after I had come back from Greece, Tom Cunliffe rang. The nights were drawing in by now, the trees were bare, and there was ice on the puddles in the yard. I was working again with the sheep, this time as a contract shepherd on a nearby Sussex farm. In contrast to my Elysian summer, I spent my days out on the hills, up to my knees in mud and driving rain, sorting lambs, foot-rotting sheep, moving electric fences. I enjoyed the work and was decently paid for it, but was troubled by a restlessness, a feeling that the chapter I had opened on the sea had come to a close before I'd had a chance to prove myself. I daydreamed that instead of grappling day after day with sodden sheep, I might have been better employed at the helm of some graceful craft, ploughing across the oceans of the world.

Tom, as you may recall, had been my teacher on the Competent Crew course, and the man who had first instilled in me a love of the sea and its boats and its language and literature.

'We've just about finished work on *Hirta*, Chris,' Tom announced, 'and she's looking magnificent. Tight as a nut, and she goes like a rocket.'

I could well believe it. *Hirta* was his boat, a vintage Bristol Channel Pilot Cutter, that he and his wife Ros had been restoring. I had seen her when I went to visit Tom for the weekend, at the end of our Isle of Wight sailing course, and had been bewitched by her classic beauty. She looked not unlike a Crabber, only much bigger and more solid and with a long graceful sheer.

'I'm getting a crew together,' Tom continued. 'We're going to sail her up to Norway and across the north Atlantic to Iceland, and eventually to Newfoundland – you know, in the footsteps of Leif Eiriksson.'

'Hell, Tom… that sounds fantastic.'

'I wouldn't put it quite like that,' he went on. 'It's going to be a beast of a journey: five months, at least. And even in summer it'll be bloody cold. There'll be icebergs up there, and bound to be a storm or two. I can't promise you plain sailing, but you're right – it'll be fun, and you'll learn a hell of a lot more than you did puddling around in the Med on that little tub of yours.'

'You mean… you mean…?' I spluttered. I wasn't sure I had heard right.

To say I was excited would be an understatement. I was staggered. This was an adventure like I'd grown up imagining an adventure to be. Tom went on to say that our voyage north would be the most unpleasant and dangerous experience I would ever be likely to have, that I would be by turns sopping wet, freezing cold, unutterably bored and frightened half to death.

'Are you on, then?' he concluded.

'Well of course I'm on,' I almost shouted.

How could I possibly resist such a tempting prospect? Perhaps I ought to mention it to Ana, but there was plenty of time for that. I listened on. The rest of the crew had already been chosen: Ros would be going, of course, which meant they'd be bringing along Hannah, their four-year-old daughter, who had effortlessly won my heart. Then there was John, a merchant-seaman shipmate of Tom's, to whom, he assured me, he'd happily trust his boat and his life; Patrick, an ex-army man who knew about sailing in the Arctic; and Mike, a teenager who had done exceptionally well on Tom's skipper course and was taking a gap year before starting an engineering degree.

I wondered what quality it was that had landed me a place among such a seasoned crew. 'Oh,' said Tom, before hanging up, 'bring your guitar. Hannah likes your songs,' and he added, as if in answer to my question, 'she thinks you're funny.'

WHEN I BROKE THE NEWS OF MY VOYAGE, Ana turned out to be a little less sanguine than I had expected. She had always accommodated my wanderlust, placing a high value on her own independence as much as mine; but was I really sure about the safety of it all? Tom had, after all, talked about storms at sea and this played on her mind. It reassured her to some extent that Ros and Hannah were going along; nothing awful would be allowed to happen to the boat while they were on board. But what if I fell off it? What if far from land we hit the sort of freak weather that was beyond even the skill of the legendary Tom Cunliffe?

I worked on through that winter with the sheep, and by the end of March, and lambing, I had enough money saved for my share of the expenses. I put the wheels in motion to see that the flock was well cared for while I was away and, in order to present my case to Ana in a better light, set to work with more enthusiasm than skill, on some long-promised home improvements. All this had the effect of keeping me well occupied, and distracting me from my seething excitement about the journey. At long last April came, and with it the eagerly awaited call from Tom to say that everything was ready for our departure.

On a grim sort of a day with a lowering grey sky and squalls of rain scudding across the Downs, Ana drove me down to Brighton Marina, where *Hirta* now lay. It all seemed full of menace and foreboding and, as we drove, it got worse and worse. We didn't say much and, at the marina, as we walked arm in arm up the quay, Ana leaned into me as much for warmth and a windbreak as for affection.

Hirta was moored at the end of the quay. I felt a frisson of pride as I saw her; her hull was deep black now with new paint, the spars – mast, bowsprit and boom – glistened with coat upon coat of oil. The brasswork gleamed, the deck was scrubbed and everywhere were well-coiled ropes, hanging from the pinrails or neatly flaked down on the deck. The sails were shackled or tied into place and ready to be raised; all in all she looked a most businesslike boat, and reassuringly well prepared for sea.

'Now, there', I said to Ana, 'is a well-found ship.'

'I suppose you're right,' she answered, just a little absently.

Hannah waved at us. She had posted herself as lookout, her little red Wellingtons and plastic mackintosh setting off her pale blonde hair. As we climbed aboard, she ran giggling in a fit of shyness to hide behind her father's legs. Ros, who had been making tea in the galley, poked her head out at the top of the companionway steps to greet us. It struck me anew what a contrast they made: Ros, slender, quiet and assured; Tom, towering above her, and with the presence of a bear in a bar room.

'Welcome aboard,' he boomed. 'Get your kit stowed. I see you've brought the guitar. Wonderful. We're having a quick cup of tea and some sticky buns to fortify us and then we'll slip the lines and get under way. The weather's not what it might be, but then it never is, is it?'

A handsome man of about thirty-five, and a gangly, mop-haired youngster with round spectacles were busy on deck lashing gas bottles into the big red dinghy. They paused for a moment to shout greetings, the former turning on a dazzling smile, which Ana returned.

'That's Patrick,' said Tom, gallantly handing Ana down into the cockpit, and then through the companionway doors to climb down the steps into the bowels of the boat.

It was good to get below and out of the cutting wind. The saloon, where a little pot-bellied stove supplied a welcome warmth, felt like a congenial place to be spending the next half-year. While Ana chatted easily to Ros, Tom's attention was held by a slight, mild-mannered man, who, while thoughtfully fingering his beard, was speculating about the probable outcome of the weather pattern that was establishing itself. 'I'm John,' he said, extending his hand, before resuming their conversation.

Soon the tea and the buns were gone, and it looked like it was time for leaving. I moved to Ana's side. We could all hear the wind screaming in the rigging, the frenzied clattering of wire stays on tin masts. It sounded nasty out there. John, with reluctance, was suggesting we might want to delay our departure, wait for better weather.

'I'd given that some thought, too,' said Tom. 'But I think we're all set, and the waiting will do more harm than the wind.'

'It's true,' said John. 'We've got to bite the bullet sometime.'

'Right, let's do it.' And Tom rose to his feet and went to start the engine.

I saw Ana off the boat, and there on the gale-lashed mole she kissed me goodbye. Feeling just a little lovelorn, I hung onto the shrouds (the tensioned ropes that support the mast on either side of the boat... and the handiest bit to cling to when leaning over the side) and waved to the dwindling figure of my girlfriend as we motored towards the harbour mouth.

'I'LL SEE YOU NEXT AUTUMN,' I shouted. But my words were whipped away by the wind, as *Hirta* shouldered her way into what looked an ominously swelling grey sea.

'THE ROUTE WE'RE TAKING', Tom announced to his crew, 'is the logical and best way to get from Brighton to Newfoundland. Our next landfall, in a week or maybe ten days at the worst, will be Norway. With the right sort of wind up our chuff we should make it to the Hardangerfjord for apple blossom time, which is one of the lesser known wonders of the world. We have a good supply of whisky to trade with the natives, which ought to see us right for a warm welcome.

'Then, when we've exhausted our credit with the Norwegians, we'll head west past the Faroe Islands, and on to Iceland, and, if ice conditions are right we can put in at

Julianahaab in Greenland. And then on amongst the bergs and growlers of the mighty north Atlantic until we hit the north coast of Vinland.'

I looked around me. Everyone else seemed to know where Vinland was except me, and perhaps Mike, who was intently studying his shoes. Vinland, it transpired, was a historic destination in the Icelandic sagas, more commonly known as Newfoundland. I was going to hear a lot about the sagas on this journey; they were a literary passion and inspiration of Tom's.

But the main point was that it was a long way... and for now the task was to get safely away from Brighton. For, not ten minutes into our voyage, the wind was already building fiercely. Hannah had disappeared below deck with Ros, leaving Tom to shout instructions from the cockpit, both hands clamped on the wheel. You couldn't help but notice that ours was the only boat on the water.

'Safety lines on!' Tom shouted through the foul weather. 'I'll keep her head to wind; get the storm jib up, quick as you can.' This is a small but heavy duty sail that is flown from the bow when the wind is really strong.

We hauled at the ropes like men demented, slithering and sliding on the bucking foredeck. The red triangle of canvas rose like a spirit from the deck and leaped into the air. Then with a thunderous crack the sail snapped into the wind and instantly tore into shreds. The remaining tatters of sail and rope thrashed and flogged in a frenzy. It felt as if poor *Hirta* were being beaten to bits.

'Kill that sail!' yelled Tom from the wheel.

I leaped to grab a snaking rope. It upped and smacked me in the head like a kick from a mule. I fell and grabbed at a stay to stop myself slipping overboard. Swiftly, Patrick, a bigger-built man than me, and far more alert to the real danger of a flogging sail, managed to quell its fury. But not before the long free end of the sail's ropes had fallen overboard and snarled up in the propeller, thus putting the engine out of action.

Tom cursed, Patrick was ashen-faced. It was humiliating for seasoned sailors like them to be caught in such a balls up so close to the land, even if none of them were culpable. For myself, I was mortified. What sort of asset was I going to be if I couldn't even grab hold of a rope? But there was no time for such reflections; Tom was shouting to us to reef the sail. This is where you loosen and then tie up the lower segments of the sail – making it all a lot smaller and therefore offering less resistance to the wind. It's one of the crucial manoeuvres, that every sailor learns, to lessen the impact of a storm.

With an alternative sail taking the place of the storm jib, and with the mainsail substantially bundled and tied (or double-reefed) we headed east, and four hours later decided to put in at Newhaven to clear the propeller. God, I thought. I hope this is not the way it's going to be all the way to Newfoundland. Summer in Greece didn't prepare me for this. There was also a worry playing on my mind. How the hell, I wondered to myself, do you go about clearing a rope from a propeller without actually diving beneath the bottom of the boat? It didn't bear thinking about.

'RIGHT CHRIS, ARE YOU READY? I'll hand you the knife once you've got that safety rope sorted out; we don't want you slicing bits off yourself by accident.'

It was Tom, leaning like the others over the side while I slid, tied to a safety line and fully clothed (for we hadn't a wetsuit and, even when immersed in water, wool still imparts a certain warmth), into the cold, cold sea. The odd thing was that I felt almost glad that I was the one to have pulled the short straw. It made me feel important and useful and redeemed that sense of guilt that maybe I could have prevented the rope slipping overboard. At least that's how I felt before the first gush of freezing water welled into my trousers, agonisingly consumed my nether parts and then made a grab for my neck. God, it was cold!

Cold sea is always better once you're fully immersed, so I dived down, groping my way along the keel until I came to the propeller. I kept my eyes shut because the water in Newhaven Harbour, as well as being cold and fast moving with the tide, was about as clear as mushroom soup. The knot, thankfully, was easy to find – a mass of thick rope wedged tight into every turn of the propeller blades, like a grotesque sinewy growth.

Clutching the keel with one hand so as not to be whooshed out to the open sea by the tide, I started cutting. To my dismay the rope had been twisted so tight by the force of the propeller that it had taken on the consistency of steel cable. I sawed feebly through a few fibres and then burst to the surface, panting and spluttering.

My shipmates looked down at me expectantly. 'Are you OK? Have you done it?' they asked.

'Very nearly,' I lied as I wheezed and honked for air, and then ducked under again.

A few more fibres, a lunge to the surface for breath. Yet more still, and another lunge for breath. I continued in this manner until my fingers and face were half frozen and my body began to quake with cold.

'I think you should come up,' Ros insisted after nearly half an hour had passed. The others had stopped asking about progress, as they too thought I should stop for a break. But it would be unthinkable to stop without finishing the job. There were just a few more fibres to go. I sawed and hacked like a man possessed and at last the tangled skeins of rope came away in my hands. Propelled by an enormous sense of achievement I burst back to the surface, where five pairs of arms helped haul me back on board and guide me down to the cabin.

I had just about managed to tug off my sodden layers of clothes and get into my arctic sleeping bag before the shivering started in earnest. I'd heard once of a man who shivered so much that he cracked a couple of ribs. Well, that's how I was shivering now. My teeth were chattering, my very bones were chattering.

'You've got a touch of hypothermia,' said Ros, cracking open a small bag of heat-producing iron filings from the ship's survival kit and passing it to me. I was unable to acknowledge the truth of what she was saying as my jaw was convulsed in violent spasms along with all the rest of my muscles. I cuddled the miracle bag that seemed somehow to be offering my body something of its lost heat.

Nor could I gesture, as I was stuffed tightly into my sleeping bag – silk filled with goose down, liner of cashmere wool, good for forty degrees below zero. Yet even so I felt that I might never get warm again, as I lay there, my body racked with convulsions. Gradually, though, a little of the warmth of life began to creep back into my body and I was able to take a couple of sips of soup and fall into a sound sleep.

I slept so deeply and so fast that not even the clattering of boots on the deck, nor the roaring of the engine, nor the rumbling of the ropes in the blocks... none of these sounds was able to rouse me to the fact that long before dawn we had put to sea. It was hours later when I slipped back into consciousness, and lay gloriously warm, listening to the sound of the water rushing along the wooden hull just inches away from my ear. When finally I emerged from my bag, the new day was well into the morning. I crept out onto the sloping deck and gazed across a blue and sunlit sea towards the white cliffs of Dover.

The wind was right and the tide was sweeping us fast along to where we would round the South Foreland and head north up through the Straits of Dover and into the English Channel. It was early in May and we were heading, by what seemed to me a circuitous route, for Vinland.

NIGHT BEGAN TO FALL and the pale cliffs of the Kent coast were replaced by distant lines of light. With the deepening of the darkness the sea too vanished and we seemed to move through a fathomless blackness, with just the glimmer of foam in our wake to place us in the firmament. High in the shrouds the red light of the port lantern shone dimly on the mainsail. A few scattered stars peeped from behind the scudding clouds. A faint silver glow on the northeast horizon intensified until a bright shard of moon rose from the dark, shook herself and began her climb into the night sky. The gale had abated and become a light wind blowing from the west, just what we wanted to drive *Hirta*, now under full press of sail, northward towards the North Sea and Scandinavia.

We all sat in the cockpit – a large sunken area on the open deck, like a big wooden bath with benches, that surrounded the wheel and compass. There was the friendly glow of a couple of cigarettes and the comforting scent of thin curls of smoke, as we talked quietly, so as not to dispel the enchantment of our first night at sea. Each of us cradled a mug of hot tea, for it can be murderous cold on the deck of a boat in the North Sea on an April night. Hannah was below, wrapped in peaceful sleep, rocked by the waves and cuddling her rag doll, Rowena.

Now the great pleasure of ocean voyaging, as opposed to day sailing, is that as the land drops away astern, all the woes and worries that afflicted you on dry land – all the things you ought to have done but have left undone, all the drab detritus and clutter of your daily existence – slough away like the old dry skin of a snake. You feel renewed and newly alive. There's nothing you can do about any of that old stuff, so you forget it and just attend to the business of navigation and survival… because getting things right on an ocean voyage in a small boat is simply a matter of life and death.

This phenomenon, which strips people down to their essence, happens every time you leave the land. And just as surely, when finally the lookout perched high up the mast shouts, 'Land ahoy!', you are overwhelmed with longing for the land, and mysteriously ready and eager again to immerse yourself in that cloying bog of cares.

Sensing all of this, we mused and chatted, sounding one another out, testing the parameters where you could and couldn't go. There was a tentative pleasure in getting to know each other in the knowledge that we were soon to be hurled together and shaken up in conditions of the weirdest intimacy. Tom had warned me that to be confined together in the cabin of a small wooden boat, tossed amongst the terrors of the open sea, has the effect of a pressure cooker. Feelings that are best left simmering beneath the surface burst forth in extremis, and have to be dealt with to make life even halfway tolerable.

Tonight, though, we took a mild and friendly interest in each other, bandied compliments, trying to show ourselves in our most appealing light, without overstepping the mark. We each sipped whisky from a mug, the traditional treat at the start of the night – and the whisky in its wonderful way warmed our hearts and our spirits.

And then it was gone midnight and a reverential silence fell for The Shipping Forecast. Like anybody else I had heard the shipping forecast before on the radio; a meaning-less almost mystical incantation, the clear, clipped tones of the BBC enunciating, 'Dover, Thames, Humber, Dogger, German Bight... Fisher, Fair Isle, Cromarty, Viking, Faroes, Southeast Iceland...' and so on; comfortingly obscure names that had suddenly become both personal and press-ing. Even its theme tune, 'Sailing By', which I had always thought rather vacuous, took on a different form, its rippling arpeggios charged with meaning and emotion.

From now on we would hear 'Sailing By' each night as we plied our way north, until we'd sailed so far that not even the BBC could reach us.

'IT'S TIME TO START the watch system,' announced Tom. 'We'll do four-hour turns, two to a watch: John, you can have Mike, and Patrick can be with Chris. As skipper I don't have a specific watch but you can call me any time, day or night.'

And thus I found myself doing ten until two in the morning, just Patrick and me alone in the cockpit while a steady wind drove us northward through the night. Patrick spoke with the softest of Scottish accents. He was an experienced sailor and beneath his gentle well-mannered exterior he was really hard, the result of years in the army. I was happy to take orders from Patrick; he knew what was going on... I knew nothing.

'Take the wheel, Chris, and keep her on that heading, zero one five, while I go forward and give the sails a tweak.'

I took the wheel and peered myopically at the dimly illuminated compass in its binnacle just inside the cabin hatchway. At that distance of about two and a half yards I couldn't quite make out the figures. This was a problem for me all the way to Vinland. What I would have to do was abandon the wheel for a moment and move forward to get a clear sight on the compass, then leap back for the wheel before the boat had moved too far off her course. Naturally by the time I got back to the wheel *Hirta* would have changed course by a few points, so I would have to dart forward again to the compass, nip back and give a tweak to the wheel, then forward again to see if I had got the adjustment right. It was far from satisfactory, but resulted in a certain sort of a zigzag progress in roughly the desired direction.

On a starry night the whole thing became easier because you could get your course more or less right, then find a star close to some fixed point on the masthead, and then keep the relation of the star constant to it. The problem, however, with this much more romantic method of navigation is that the stars are also sailing in a circular fashion across the bowl of the night and if you fix on just one star you end up going round in a great circle. So you must change your star every five or ten minutes to keep on track.

On that first watch, as Patrick beavered about on the foredeck in the dark, I listened to the creaking of the mast and boom, the whistling of the wind in the shrouds and the rushing of the waves against the hull. And I thought how wonderful it was to be here out of sight of land, and heading for Vinland.

At ten to two I went below to make tea for the next watch and wake them up. It just remained to write down in the log what had or had not happened during the watch – changes of wind direction, course, anything of interest spotted, and then slip thankfully into my sleeping bag to sleep. And how I slept... the rocking of a boat and the sound of water slipping along the planking are the most wonderful aids to tumbling deep into sleep and dreaming. Unfortunately, though, it never lasts.

At six, in the light of a grey dawn with the rain streaming from a sky the colour of slate, the grinning face of Mike, the boat's boy by virtue of his being the youngest member of the crew, appeared with a mug of tea. 'It's a horrible day,' he observed. 'And it's time you were up and in it. I'm going to bed.'

I rolled out of my bunk, and before it had time to get cool, Mike rolled into it. This peculiar form of intimacy is known as 'hot-bunking'.

THOSE FIVE DAYS ON THE NORTH SEA, my first proper voyage, passed in something of a blur. Mostly there was little to see but rolling walls of water, sometimes grey, sometimes brown, and occasionally green, bearing down on us in endless procession. Sometimes they glinted or shone with pale sunlight, but more often they were opaque and brooding, and then all of a sudden the midday sun would break through the mists and the sea would turn a deep pellucid blue, sparkling and glittering.

There was a curious soporific feel to the days, the long hours passing without any particular interruption or event. The watch system was relaxed during the day, and we would take a trick at the helm whenever we felt the inclination, or busy ourselves with the constant tasks of whipping and splicing ropes. On land it would have been too tedious to bear, but here at sea I seemed to enter a completely different state of mind, the consequence of a hint of sea-

sickness and not nearly enough sleep. I never got an unin-
terrupted night's sleep; three or four hours was the longest
the watches would allow you. We would doze during the
day to make up for lost hours, but could never quite shake
off a heavy-lidded torpor.

This had the effect of blunting the intellect a little and
enhancing the feelings. I'm moved too easily anyway, but
on the high seas I found myself constantly brought to the
edge of tears, by the simplest of things: a sudden burst of
sunlight from behind a cloud, or a pleasing notion, or a
particularly vivid thought of a loved one. And the simple act
of standing at the wheel, watching the red sails billowing
into the sky, and feeling the great black hull surging swiftly
through the waves, filled me with ineffable delight.

Tom, as skipper, was constantly occupied with the maintenance of his beloved boat and by extension the safety
and well-being of the crew. He would strip down the diesel
engine and clean the injectors, cast an eye on the wear
and tear of the running gear (the ropes and sails), which
suffered from constant chafing, and stay aware of our
course and position, as well as finding useful things for us
to do.

Ros looked after the galley, keeping us well fed and
happy. Curry, which she did well, has an almost supernatu-
ral effect on a wet, cold crew on a nasty night at sea. And
for much of the day she would be teaching and reading to
Hannah. The rest of us would take it in turns at the helm,
trim the sails, and do whatever tasks Tom had allotted to

us. And on the odd occasions when the sun deigned to appear, everyone would rush onto the deck and try to fix our position with a sextant.

Mike, John and Patrick were making use of the trip to brush up their navigation techniques, taking advantage of Tom's considerable skill. This was long before the days of GPS, and an ability to use the sextant was essential for ocean navigation, quite apart from the fact that mastery of this traditional instrument was an art in itself. Navigators have relied upon this beautiful device of gleaming brass for hundreds of years, and just to slip one out of its case and hold it to your eye casts you into the unbroken spell of time that links you to Columbus, Magellan or Henry the Navigator.

The ideal time to take a sun sight on a sextant is at noon, although of course this is not always possible, as the sun is not necessarily shining at noon, especially in the dismal latitudes towards which we were heading. In theory, though, you can take a sight at other times of the day as long as the sun is visible above the horizon and you have an accurate watch. But if it isn't noon, it complicates the calculations no end.

On our boat, if the sun were visible just before noon, the navigators would gather on deck and prepare their instruments. Then, as the moment of the zenith approached, they would adjust the ingenious little smoked mirrors to catch the exact moment the sun ceased its climb and started to drop. That was exact celestial noon, and the figures so accurately etched into the brass arms and arcs of the sextant could now be read off and entered into the calculations. This was also an opportunity to check the accuracy of the chronometers, i.e. our watches.

Next everyone would tumble down the ladder to the chart table, where there would be a frenzy of calculations and poring over navigation tables. Then there would be such sucking of pencils, and muttering and leafing through pages grey with tan and cosine and sine, and date coefficients and declination and other unfathomable logarithms, until the final calculation was made and an estimate of our position arrived at.

Although I dearly wanted to be involved, there were only three sextants on board and it became obvious that if I were to muscle in on the masterclasses it would all become a bit of a scrum. For the first couple of days, I graciously bowed out. But on the third day the desire to navigate got too much for me; I cracked, and, seizing a moment in the afternoon when everyone else had returned to their bunks or allotted tasks, I crept up on deck with Tom's sextant and took my own sight. It wasn't a particularly opportune moment to take a reading, but it would have to do. Unhurriedly and with all the figures at my disposal, I busied myself down at the chart table all on my own with the complex calculations.

My deliberations moved inexorably towards their conclusion, until at last, panting mentally from the excess of mathematical gymnastics, I had the numbers. Excitedly,

I drew in my lines across the chart, trying vainly to ignore the little copses of half-rubbed-out pencil marks that indicated everybody else's approximation of our whereabouts. These were quite closely grouped.

However, as my pencil slid along the ruler towards the spot where it would intersect with my first plotted line, the truth began to dawn on me that things were not as they seemed. I removed the ruler and stared, brow furrowed, at the crossed pencil lines. Either everybody else was wildly out – which seemed to me the more likely option – or else I myself had slipped up badly. For my estimate of our position, far from being about fifty nautical miles southwest of the northern tip of Denmark, as the other navigators tended to agree, had us high and dry on the top of a prominent hill just to the south of Scunthorpe.

Hurriedly I rubbed out the lines. It seemed best to keep this disappointing discovery to myself. In fact, I resolved to leave the sextant work in the future to the eager navigators, for it was hard to imagine a useful result coming from my own offbeat deliberations. So far out to sea, though, you never know exactly where you are, anyway. And it doesn't really matter that much. It's only when you draw close to land that you need an exact position, in order not to pile your boat onto the bricks, as Tom would have it.

Although I never quite got the hang of sextant maths, Tom did show me how you can get a rough idea of where you are by 'dead reckoning'. This is a matter of plotting your course onto the chart. You have to make allowances for tides and currents, magnetic variations, leeway (which is the way that the wind blows you a little sideways off your intended track), and your speed, which you ascertain by streaming a device known as a log – a primitive instrument with a propeller on it that you throw into the sea way behind the wash of the boat. You plot all this information, along with changes of course, wind speed and direction in the logbook, and on the basis of it you have some idea of where you are... although – unless you're very slick – not much.

DURING ALL OF THOSE FIVE LONG DAYS sailing northwards to Norway, we saw no sign of land and, apart from the odd distant ship, there was not much to see on the sea, either, apart from a few birds.

I bemoaned this to Tom one day, or at least mused aloud about the monotony of the sea compared with the variety of the land with its ever-changing views of rocks, flowers and trees. But he wouldn't have any of it. 'Birds', he declared, 'are the flowers of the sea. They're the living element of the seascape; they give it colour and personality and endless variety. There's not an ocean-going sailor who doesn't care about birds. Even if you didn't give a fig for birds before you went to sea, you soon come to love them. They're your constant companions and you get to know everything there is to know about them.'

And sure enough, the longer we were at sea, the more I came to see the truth of this. The presence of birds was enough to dispel our loneliness and fill us with fascination. Tom and Ros, Patrick and John knew all there was to know about them and could recognise who and what they were when they were no more than distant specks far away among the waves. We all had our favourites. Mine was the fulmar, a fat little grey and white gull with an amiable disposition and a quizzical look – a companionable sort of bird that you felt might be sticking close to the boat for the company rather than just the search for food. There were plenty of fulmars wheeling around amongst the waves as we sailed up the North Sea, though as we journeyed north I transferred my allegiance to the gannet, which started to make its appearance in ever greater numbers.

Gannets are bigger than fulmars and, oddly enough, given our metaphor for frenzied gluttony, longer and more slender and graceful. Gannets dive spectacularly from a great height; they fold up as they hit the water and down as far as two hundred feet they can give a fish a run for its money. To my mind that should class them as amphibians, although this is not generally conceded. But to see a flock of gannets fishing, plummeting from sixty feet up in the air, racing amongst the schools of fish and then launching themselves from the waves again for another high dive, is one of the unforgettable sights of the sea. And then there's the strangeness of the gannet's cry, for it sounds just like a raven... a sound you associate more with the loneliness of heather-clad moorland than with the rolling wastes of the ocean. 'Gark... gark,' they cry.

Gannets fly vast distances but go home to their nests most nights for a kip. Fulmars are a tougher lot. They are pelagic, which means they live almost entirely at sea. They will go for months, even years, without touching land; indeed the only time they do touch land is when they lay their eggs and rear their young. In the case of the fulmar, she doesn't lay her first eggs until she's eight years old, so once a chick leaves the nest it spends the next eight years of life at sea. It's hard to imagine this companionable creature spending so many years with nowhere to perch for comfort and warmth other than the waves of a high sea.

'If we were off in the southern oceans,' Tom told me one morning, 'you'd see albatross, and just the sight of an albatross will wrench your heartstrings. They're big and graceful and they range over all the oceans of the world, and they live in terrible loneliness as if there really were a curse upon them, just like in the poem.' Sadly, albatross rarely come north of the line, so we didn't get to spot one, and I fear that a certain restlessness has now descended on my soul – in that special place where we keep our thwarted ambitions.

Along with the birdwatching and sextant studies, Tom and most of the crew had a passion for the Vinland Sagas, the ancient Icelandic tales of Leif Eiriksson's discovery of Vinland. Indeed, Tom's expedition had been premised in part on a desire to follow the journey of Leif Eiriksson, who in about 1000 AD set out from from Iceland for

Greenland, but was blown by storms way to the southwest. As a consequence, Leif was the first European to discover the Americas, which he called Vinland. The saga about his voyage recounts at great length the dastardly exploits of – and I am not making these names up – the unappetising Ragnar Hairybreeches, the loathsome Eirik Bloodaxe and our hero Leif's mother-in-law, the redoubtable lady Thorbjorg Ship-Bosom.

For myself, I was never entirely taken with Viking saga and its raw-boned fare. Instead, I buried my head in a volume of Edward Lear's nonsense verse, which I found in the ship's library. I began with 'The Dong with the Luminous Nose', which I learnt by heart during a day's watch, to entertain Hannah. But it was 'The Jumblies' that captured the imagination of everyone on board, with its chorus:

Far and few, far and few,
Are the lands where the Jumblies live;
Their heads are green, and their hands are blue,
And they went to sea in a Sieve.

Being a vintage wooden boat, *Hirta* had a tendency to leak in a heavy sea, so the appositeness of this was lost on nobody. Indeed, it wasn't long before most of the crew could reel off quotes for appropriate occasions as well as chant the chorus. And so the time fairly zipped by – and in five days we had reached Norwegian waters.

This was, according to Tom, 'good passage-making'. We had averaged roughly five knots, which is about the speed you back your car into the garage, or toil uphill on a bicycle slowly. Now you might well consider this and conclude that such a journey is a waste of time, and on the surface of things you might be right. It's an expensive form of travel, too; during five days at sea we had probably consumed enough whisky, Marsbars, tea, canned food and diesel to buy each of us a flight. And most of the time we were rather wet and cold... and during the first twenty-four hours almost everyone was stricken by seasickness.

It is undoubtedly a madness. And yet I remember reading in Antoine de Saint Exupéry's 'Wind, Sand and Stars' of how the author once told a Bedouin camel driver that in his flying machine he could do in two hours the journey that would take a camel caravan ten days. The Bedouin pensively scratched his aquiline nose, and then looked deep into the aviator's eyes. 'Why', he asked quietly, 'would a person want to do that?'

I'm with the Bedouin every time here. I'd plump any day for exploring the beauty that the world has to offer. I know people who have never slept a night beneath the stars. In fact, there are probably people who have never climbed a hill, nor swum in a river or a lake. It's time they did.

At last we saw to the north a thin grey line a little more distinct than the horizon. As the hours passed and the breeze drove us on, the line became clearer and finally resolved itself into the jagged cliffs and forested islands of western Norway. We had only been five days at sea, but even so there was a tremendous desire to set foot on dry land. There are those who would have it that sailing is like banging your head against a wall: it's only good when you stop. And it's hard to deny that one of the greater pleasures is pulling in to a quiet bay or a harbour at the end of an ocean passage. To walk in the woods, to climb a hill or go to a bar or a bakery.

As we slipped behind the outer islands and entered the more sheltered archipelago, the sea became calmer, and *Hirta* churned along unimpeded by the waves of the open sea. We lay around on the deck oohing and aahing at the beauty of the place… the little green valleys, the cliffs and waterfalls and huge ranges of snowy mountains all reflected in the deep, still waters. But the serenity of the scene was, apparently, quite deceptive. According to Tom there were winds that could all of a sudden rush down the mountains and knock a boat like ours clean over. Katabatic winds, he called them, that could spring at you from the still and silent landscape like a wild beast breaking cover. And they could rush the other way, too (these were called anabatic winds), knocking boats like skittles as they raced from the water straight up the mountainside.

We mulled this over silently. Fortunately neither wind made a showing that day, and we moved on uneventfully through the baffling maze of islands and fjords that hide the entrance to the port city of Bergen. And there we did what sailors do, which is go to a bar and drink beer, our faces full of wind and our bodies swaying with the memory of waves. Norway was ruinously expensive back then, and the beer was well beyond our modest means, but we had to have it. We felt special, in the way that you do when you come in off the sea, or down off a mountain; we existed on a slightly different plane from those around us.

Not long after, we slipped our moorings and headed south, and after a day of cruising easily in the flat water of the fjords, we dropped anchor in the bay of Norheimsund, a little town on the Hardangerfjord. It was apple blossom time, and there is simply nothing, as Tom had said, quite like the Hardangerfjord in apple blossom time. The fjord itself is a place of heart-stopping beauty, with its sheets of deep calm water spreading inland for a hundred miles among idyllic valleys, backed by snow-capped mountains. In early summer this effect is heightened by the glowing mists of pure white blossoms that shine from the apple orchards as if bright patches of snow had lingered in the warm green valleys, and beneath the trees the meadows are a dense carpet of wild flowers. It made you wonder why anyone would want to leave such a place, especially to head out on the desperate sea route to Vinland.

We were in no hurry to leave the fjords, as we were waiting for the late summer melting of the ice pack, so we wandered, wafted by gentle breezes, from harbour to harbour and fjord to fjord, marvelling at the beauty of it all. We ate pollock, because it was too expensive to buy anything to eat in Norway, and the fjords were alive with pollock. We kept a line trailing from the stern of the boat, and we lived off pollock stew and pollock curry and pollock fried and baked and boiled. To accompany it, we drank whisky from the ship's stores, as we couldn't afford the beer. Pollock and whisky... well, you could do worse.

And then one night, moored to the fish dock in some wind-blasted town way out in the outlying islands, we were invaded by drunks who had smelled the whisky. The Norwegians have a weakness for this sort of thing; it's the long gloomy Nordic winter coupled with a general Scandinavian propensity for the bottle, a hangover no doubt from the Vikings. The first inkling of the drunks' presence was a crate of beer which appeared through the skylight and then was lovingly lowered on to the saloon table. After this display of good intent we had to invite them down, and there they proceeded to make ruinous inroads into our whisky supply, while regaling us with incomprehensible stories in Norwegian. Eventually Tord, their ringleader, stumbled over to the galley to see what we were going to eat.

'Vot is dis?' he asked, poking a pollock with distaste.

'That', said Ros defensively, 'is what we're going to have for supper. It's pollock.'

'Pollocks!' spluttered Tord, his great beery red face aghast. 'Pollocks? Nobody eat pollocks. I tell you not even cats don't eat pollocks. Why you eat that fish?'

'Well it doesn't cost anything,' countered Ros. 'There are plenty of pollocks in the fjords.'

Sobered a little by thoughts of our desperate diet, Tord sat down, took a big slug of whisky, and said: 'I get you some proper think to eat. I work in der meat biznis.' And after another hour or two – the sort of session you wish had never got started – he and his cronies finally crawled ashore, leaving us to slump crapulously into our berths.

The next morning, when we had a mind to continue sleeping, there came a stumble and a thump, some feverish shuffling and a whispered oath. It was Tord coming back, as he had promised. The skylight darkened (it gets light at about two in the morning in June this far north) and the familiar beery face peered in and guffawed. With a crash a heavy piece of unidentifiable meat hit the saloon table... then another... and another... and finally a fourth.

'Ho... vid dis stuff you don't haf to eat no more pollocks. Open up de door; I need some more drinking...'

We weighed this option up. There was not a man among us who felt inclined to continue the drinking session with our benefactor... but then there lay in a heap on the table four enormous legs of smoked mutton. This was proper Viking fare – they had been big sheep and their legs would do us all the way across to Vinland without the need to troll for more pollock. To take a drink or two with Tord was clearly a moral obligation. Tom dug up the loose floorboard and fished forth another couple of bottles of whisky... and off we went again. It transpired, in the light of the illuminating conversation that ensued, that Tord had nicked the mutton from the meat works where he was employed. It didn't matter much anyway, he said, because he had just been given the boot... oddly enough for drunkenness and pilfering.

The smoked mutton, shaved thin with a hasp knife, was the most delicious thing you could imagine. Tord had at a stroke raised the gastronomic level of our journey from desperate to something close to gourmand.

For some reason which escapes me now, the four legs of mutton were hung in the heads. The heads, as nautically-minded readers will be aware, is the boat's lavatory. Ours was a tiny curved compartment containing a small porcelain bowl decked with a baffling array of levers and plungers. On the wall, now unfortunately obscured by the mutton, were the instructions that told you the order in which these things had to be operated and how... and, to a certain extent, why.

In no time at all it seemed that May had given way to June, and July was looming. It was surely time to cut loose from the tiny and hospitable harbour towns where we had moored and throw ourselves once again upon the mercy of the open sea. Yet, although we all claimed to be champing at the bit to be off, there was a discernible note of reluctance amongst us sailermen (as the locals called us) to wrench ourselves away from our new-found friends – whole families who had welcomed us into their homes – and cast ourselves on the mercy of the north Atlantic. So we stalled for a few days by putting in at one of the outermost islands, ostensibly to make some small repair, but in reality storing up a last bit of comfort from the warm, dry land before committing ourselves to the horrible icy cold and danger that we all knew lay ahead. The island was too small to have cars. It had a toy-town port and a cluster of coloured wooden cottages linked by neatly tended gravel paths. A dozen or so sodden sheep looked at us without interest, and the postman, with his little trolley, kept his head down against the wind and rain and ignored us altogether. It didn't seem quite real.

As we left this last reach of land, we listened gloomily to the forecasts: 'West Viking, Faroes, Southeast Iceland, westerly force seven increasing eight occasionally nine, driving rain...'

'Right on the nose,' grumbled Tom. 'Just our luck; the prevailing winds ought to be out of the east at this time of year. It'll be tough setting out into the teeth of that... but I think we've got to go.'

And thus we left the safety of the fjords and set course to the west and out into the trackless wastes of the North Atlantic. Neither Mike nor I had ever sailed across a proper ocean before. The English Channel and North Sea, for all their bluster and rage, were a municipal duckpond compared to the vastness of the ocean we were about to navigate. Perhaps in recognition of this I slumped over the rail and vomited copiously to leeward into the grey water; further forward, I saw Mike was doing the same thing.

John emerged from below with mugs of hot tea and, catching sight of the pair of us, turned pale, banged the tea down and dived for the last available space at the rail. Vomiting is like yawning: you see somebody else doing it and immediately you want to do it yourself. Tom, striking a seamanlike pose, and Patrick at the wheel, grinned knowingly at one another as they sipped their tea and helped themselves to our ration of chocolate digestive biscuits. Everybody's different: Patrick had never been seasick in his life; Tom was much like the rest of us, prone to sickness the first twenty-four hours at sea, but sensibly dosed on seasick pills.

Being sick is rarely agreeable, but when you are on the first leg of an ocean voyage, and you are wondering why you are there anyway, it somehow makes everything even more ghastly than it already is. And it was pretty ghastly however you looked at it. With the mainsail up and sheeted tightly in, we were motoring, as there was not much wind yet and what there was was dead against us. The sea was unrelieved grey and there was a nasty chop crossing the swell that was coming in from the high winds to the west. Hence the vomiting: the motion of the boat was horrible. Behind us stretched for half a mile or so our track of flat water and bubbles, punctuated by swiftly dissipating dollops of vomit. The Pollock will enjoy that, I thought miserably to myself.

There's not a great deal you can do when seasickness hits, except wait it out in the knowledge that it'll soon be over. For me, pills and wristbands just dull the ache and block the reflex to heave. But mercifully, after a few hours, the worst of it fades and a bit of energy and optimism returns, like welcome gusts of fresh air. Chores become manageable rather than heroic endeavours and small pleasures take on a special sweetness – the warmth of the first sip of a mug of tea, before the wind and the spray instantly turn it to ice; the deliciousness of the chocolate spread thin on the top of a digestive biscuit; the peaty burn and the welling of inner warmth that comes with a sip of whisky; the comforting sound of 'Sailing By' and the shipping forecast; the warmth in Ros's voice below as she read Hannah a story, and Hannah's own absorbing accounts of the excitement of each day.

Night fell… or rather it didn't fall, this being summer up towards the Arctic Circle. There was just an intensifying for a couple of hours of the various greys which seemed to compose our world. There were no stars to steer by, so I was bobbing back and forth between the binnacle and the wheel, while Patrick busied himself below with some charts. It was too cold to sit the whole four-hour watch on deck, so we took it in turns to go below and thaw out by the little pot-bellied stove that warmed the saloon. The rain had stopped and the wind had come round a little to the north, which meant that we could sail more or less on the course we wanted to get to Iceland.

Hirta was heeled well over, slicing smoothly now through the waves; the choppy sea had calmed with the onset of night, making her motion far less unpleasant. Recovered by now from my bout of seasickness, I was enjoying the pull of the wooden wheel and peering into the twilight and thinking how lovely the land would be when we reached it. Reykjavik... I knew nothing about the town and had never expected to visit it. In fact, Iceland itself had a magical ring to it. But eclipsing this by a long way was the thought of sailing to the New World. Can anything ever beat that for romance? I had never been to Newfoundland or Canada or even America before, and had never felt particularly drawn to. Though in a way that hardly mattered: it was the journey that was the thing... to buy a ticket and get on a plane was all very well, but to navigate your way across the perilous ocean, driven by the winds in the centuries-old manner. Well, it was one hell of a way to get to a place.

'Hey Patrick,' I called, lonely at the helm and eager for a little improving conversation. 'What are you doing up there on the deck?' Patrick was lashed by his safety harness to the mast, and slithering about with the bucking and rolling of the boat, making the most minute adjustments to the unfathomable array of ropes that constituted *Hirta*'s running gear.

'I'll be with you in a minute,' he gasped as he panted and puffed at the hauling of some particularly weighty lift. 'Bring her up on the wind a touch, will you? ... While I get this throat purchase tightened up.'

Obediently I heaved a little on the wheel, and *Hirta* lost her speed, her sails flapping uselessly as she lay head to wind.

'Right, that'll do… Pay off again and we'll see how she goes…'

I spun the wheel back, the boat heeled as she caught the wind again the boat heeled and surged forward just the tiniest bit more swiftly than before. Patrick lurched back into the cockpit, wiped the spray from his face with his hand, and wedged himself in beside me.

'Is it really worth it, Pat… all that buggering about you do up there?'

He looked at me kindly and grinned.

'Well, it keeps me out of trouble… and it sort of makes me happy.' He looked up squinting at the billowing red sails, black against the grey of the arctic night.

'Wait a minute… no, look at the staysail. See where the front of it is slack? Well, that's because the jib is curling the wind round and spilling it onto that bit, so the staysail is having less effect in driving us on. Now, if I slacken off this rope here just the littlest bit… like this…' he grunted as he slipped a loop from the catch, or cleat, beside the cockpit, let it run a couple of inches, and then cleated it up again. 'Now the staysail's full of wind and tight; the ship's working just that little bit more efficiently.'

'OK,' I said. 'I see.'

'And the thing is,' continued Patrick, rather pleased to be able to impart this nugget of arcane nautical information, 'when you're sailing twenty-four hours a day and seven days a week, the tiniest bit more efficiency can make a big difference to your journey time. At full speed we're doing about seven knots,* so if you can up that by just a quarter of a knot, you're really getting somewhere. Also it's a matter of pride: you want your boat to be sailing as good as she can. And what's more important, you want everyone else to see you're doing the thing right.'

I peered into the pale cold light, where not the slightest speck or flicker of movement denoting any other vessel could be seen.

'Not out here, of course not,' he continued, 'though when Tom comes up the first thing he'll look at is the sails, and if they're not pulling as they should he'll think we're a bunch of farmers… if you'll excuse the expression.' Patrick grinned at this and slapped me playfully on the back.

'Here, give me the wheel for a spell and I'll see if I can't make something approximating a straight course.'

I slipped down the companionway into the warmth of the galley and boiled a kettle for some tea and smeared some marmalade onto a handful of digestives. It's scarcely documented the comfort that can be derived from this unlikely combination of raw materials. But they played

---

* A knot, incidentally, is one nautical mile per hour… and a nautical mile is a bit longer than a land mile, being one sixtieth of one degree of latitude – also referred to as as a minute. Knowing this, you can calculate, in case you've ever wondered, the circumference of the earth: it's sixty times three hundred and sixty… or twenty-one thousand, six hundred nautical miles.

a big part in the simple happiness that Patrick and I shared, munching and sipping as *Hirta*, all her sails full-bellied, taut and pulling, surged through the towering seas towards the distant New World to the west. Below, everybody else was wrapped in the sweet comfort of sleep while Patrick and I, in hushed tones despite the rushing and roaring of the waves and the wind, exchanged views on the subjects of war and women and the way to live a rewarding life.

We put in to Iceland because it's not every day you find yourself high up in those latitudes, and we had a yen to visit the place. But also because Tom wanted to consult the experts on the Greenland ice pack to see if we could chance an approach, and the ice monitoring station was in Reykjavik.

There wasn't a marina for yachts in those days in Reykjavik, so we tied up at the fish dock, which (as you'd expect) smelled nauseatingly of fish, with heavy overtones of diesel. But if the truth be told we didn't smell too good ourselves, and we were pleased to have anywhere at all to dock after a couple of weeks at sea on the passage from Bergen. What we all needed was a drink... and a bath.

Now the first of these was harder to find, as although Iceland had won independence from Denmark back in

1944, the draconian drinking laws imposed by the colonial power seemed still to be in operation. The only place you could buy a bottle of even the mildest liquor was the state booze monopoly... I forget the Icelandic term... and this unappetising establishment was only open at times when normal working folk had no possibility of getting to it. On the odd occasion when it was open, there were long, long queues of shamefaced Icelanders, shuffling along in the bone-crunching cold out on the street. When you finally made it to the counter, you had your identification checked by the sort of humourless, boot-faced assistants you'd expect to find running the show in a funeral parlour. The simple joy of just slipping out and buying a special bottle of wine to share with a loved one or some friends just wasn't in it. No wonder these people were driven to distil their own grog at home.

The laws were relaxed if you were going to have something to eat, so we ended up at a pizzeria, and a very good pizzeria it was, too. The speciality of the house, and the dish that has made the place for me ever memorable, was horse pizza... that is to say, a pizza which, along with the more traditional tomato and mozzarella and oregano, had horse on it. Horse can be a little on the fibrous side, but is much appreciated by the Icelanders, who are the most pragmatic of people.

In terms of personal hygiene things had come a long way since the days of Ragnar Hairybreeches, for even the most cursory reading of the sagas indicates that fastidiousness in matters of cleanliness did not figure high with Vikings. For us things were bearable so long as we stayed within a certain radius of the fish dock, but as we moved further afield we became horribly conscious of the unspeakable miasma that followed us. In the horse pizzeria, for example, we had not failed to notice a certain ripple of disdain amongst the other customers.

The reason for our disgusting state (and I do not include the much more fastidious and wholesome Ros and Hannah in this) is that it was just too damn cold at sea to wash. The only man amongst us who was bold enough to strip off and wash in a bucket on deck was Patrick... and that was because Patrick had been in the army for years and was hard as a brick. The rest of us sort of let things slide and, as a consequence, each of us was encrusted in a layer of sweat and dirt, trapped inside damp wool, unwashed socks and underwear that was best not mentioned.

Within hours of landing, Ros had managed to find the public baths, and we all trooped along armed with lotions and potions and unguents and sundry instruments – abrasive cloths, scrubbing brushes, pumice stones and sponges. The public baths in Reykjavik were, it turned out, pretty special – a great steaming hot lake, heated by geothermal energy. There was a huge glass wall that you could dive beneath and come out in the chilly open air amongst the crowds of happy Icelanders, gaily disporting themselves in the steamy waters. For it seemed that, at any one time, half the population of the city was in there.

We soon discovered that going to the baths was about the most fun to be had in the city. Keeping clean seemed to be a national obsession. So we, too, wallowed in cleanliness; we scrubbed up like cherubs and came out of there pink and gleaming. Sometimes we would go there as often as three times a day, perhaps in the clearly erroneous belief that the cleaner we got, the longer it would last us on the next leg of our journey.

It seemed we were going to be in Iceland for at least a week – anything to put off the awful inevitability of our next stint at sea. So I decided to head off and see something of the island. I stuffed some dried cod and some bread and chocolate inside my sleeping bag... and of course a slab of the ubiquitous mutton... slung it over my shoulder and trudged off along the road that leads north out of Reykjavik. I didn't know where I was going – I didn't even have a map of Iceland – but I was young then, and full of confidence that one road or another would lead me back to my friends and the boat.

Iceland, it appeared, was an elemental sort of a place, warmed by fire and steam, but lashed ceaselessly by fierce winds, a part of the earth that had remained more or less the way things were before the fishes had crawled from the sea and started their long journey to becoming people.

I saw geysers, pools of evil-smelling sulphurous sludge that boiled and bubbled in a sinister way and then all of a sudden ejaculated a plume of hot smelly water into the sky. You don't get more elemental than that, I thought to myself. Then I found myself at Gullfoss, which is a water-fall, colossal beyond dreams, that filled the dark, treeless country around with drifting mists and fearful noise.

But most wonderful of all was Thingvellir, the site of the Althing, the first Norse parliament. Here was a deep quietness, and a mystery such as I have never experienced anywhere else. It was a curious landscape lying between a rocky fault line and a shallow lake; everywhere were still clear pools and utter silence. The only building was a little white wooden church down near the lake, the only sound the haunting cry of the arctic tern, which occasionally you would spot, hovering over the pools like a delicate white swallow. I sat for long hours as evening fell, completely bewitched by the sheer strangeness of the place.

Later, hitching back towards Reykjavik, I was driven along the shore of a fjord. Steep green fields ran down to the edge of the furious wind-lashed water.

'That's my uncle's place,' said Gudrun, my driver, a stocky young woman with widely spaced green eyes and straggly blonde hair. 'He's been trying to set up a free-range chicken farm for years, but the chickens keep getting blown off the hill and into the fjord.'

'I'm not surprised,' I said, thinking about the curious, crabbed gait of the few chickens I had seen who were braving the elements. 'Back there on the road there were times when I could hardly stand up against the wind myself; it must be hell for a hen. So how is your uncle dealing with the problem?'

'He ties them to rocks,' she replied. 'The rocks are big enough so the wind can't blow the chicken away, and yet small enough so that the chicken can drag them about. Look, there's one over there.'

I turned to where she was pointing and watched, entranced, as a fine speckled-white hen dragged a rock laboriously up the hill through the grass, occasionally lifted bodily and tumbled back by the wind. Two others soon hobbled after her. These people are survivors, I thought to myself. Survivors and stickers and lateral thinkers.

Getting a lift heading back towards Reykjavik, I was overtaken by a dust storm. The world disappeared in a whirling brown mist and I emerged caked from head to toe in the finest volcanic dust. This gave me an excuse to go and wallow some more in the public pool before I rejoined the boat, where Ros had cooked us up a stew of horse, and the news was that we were putting to sea the following morning.

We were about to embark on the last, the longest and by far the most dangerous leg of the journey.

LOST AT SEA

NOT LONG AFTER we left Iceland the wind dropped altogether and the sea calmed to a long glassy swell – the ocean equivalent of rolling prairie land. We had turned on the engine and were chugging at a steady pace with the chill light breeze, created by our forward motion, competing with a rare burst of sunshine. It was one of those interludes where all the men coincided on the deck: Patrick and Tom checking their sextants, John manning the cockpit, while Mike and I lolled about for a few moments absorbing a little of the sun's wan rays.

This was not exactly sunbathing; you'd have been a fool to take off your heavy weather gear, gloves and woolly hat, but even the palest of suns peering feebly through a lowering arctic sky can impart a certain warmth to body and spirits. There was a perceptible change of mood on the boat, a light-heartedness that seemed to spread and infect us all. You'd hear bursts of song, snatches of poetry and the most inane jokes.

Hannah appeared on deck dolled up in thick layers of wool topped off by the red mackintosh and wellies. She was clutching Rowena, whom she placed carefully inside a coil of rope near the cabin door, while she arranged a new bed for her. Behind her emerged Ros with a tray of tea and some flapjacks that she and Hannah had just taken from the stove. She sat with us on the edge of the cockpit, enjoying a rare moment of relaxation while we polished off the plateful. Throughout, though, she kept one eye on Hannah and the other on the surrounding sea, scanning it for the first signs of the change that we all knew would be coming. For a calm does not last long in the north Atlantic, and although there was a feeling of relaxation and ease, there was also a sense, not quite of dread, but of anticipation.

On we ran towards the west across the mirror-like surface of the ocean, surging over the great hills of the swell. We shivered and, for a little warmth, turned our faces away from the headwind, and slipped our gloved hands beneath our armpits; you never put your hands in your pockets on a boat, as you never know when you might need them in a hurry.

The gentlest of breezes was growing, fanning in dark patches across the smooth surface of the swell, but coming, predictably enough, from almost dead ahead. This made the headwind stronger, and consequently colder. Ros gathered up the now shivering Hannah and went below, followed by everyone else, leaving me alone at the wheel. They shut the companionway doors, to keep the heat in, with just a little gap at the top through which I could almost see the compass. I was steering 285 degrees supposedly, west by northwest.

Supper was served; a good idea to eat during a period of calm. I enjoyed the feeling of being alone on deck listening to the clatter of crockery and the pleasing sounds of people eating together, talking and laughing. Even nicer was to be at the helm alone at night, while all the others, except Patrick, who would be busy at his unfathomable tasks with the ropes and sails, lay deep in sleep. It gave me a wonderful feeling of responsibility, of steering my friends safely through the night.

Patrick relieved me when he had eaten his fill, and I went below into the warmth of the cabin. My face burned as I shed the heavy canvas coat – Swedish army surplus, which protected me through the foulest weather – and sat down to assuage my raging appetite. Constantly being cold makes you very hungry.

When I returned to the deck, tearing myself away from the warm fug of the cabin and the pleasures of after-dinner conversation, that gentlest of breezes had become an icy wind. 'Here, take the wheel, will you, Chris,' said Patrick as I gloved up, thin woollen gloves inside heavy mittens. 'I'm going forward to trim up the sails. I've had to bear away a little; see if you can make two seven five and keep the sails drawing.'

I settled happily to the wheel, standing astride in front of it and holding on to the spokes behind my back. It was a good feeling, bowing your knees with the bounding motion of the boat and heading into the grey twilight of an arctic night. There was, though, a solidly ominous bank of clouds building darkly to the west, and by the time Patrick slid back into the cockpit the wind had freshened strongly, bringing with it a stinging sleet and a nasty steep chop to the waves. It looked like we were heading for a storm, and fast.

Hirta heeled hard over as Patrick sheeted in the sails, and our pleasant afternoon of calm was over. He leaned down, switched off the engine and the sounds of the sea and the old boat reasserted themselves: the thump and hiss as the bow burst into each wave, the creaking and straining of the boom, the whistling of the fresh breeze amongst the shrouds, the sort of sounds that imprint themselves for ever on your very soul. By eleven o'clock we were being battered by a ceaseless procession of fierce waves, and the wind that earlier had been whistling was nearer now to howling as *Hirta* shouldered her way through the unrelenting seas.

'This is more like it,' yelled Patrick, wiping the stinging spray from his eyes. 'Now we're making some real progress.'

I grinned at him in uncertain connivance as I cowered from the blast, teeth chattering, in the shelter of the cabin door. It looked to me as if *Hirta* was taking a bit of a beating, but I can't deny that hammering as we were into the teeth of the rising storm was pretty exciting, and if Patrick reckoned it was alright, then it probably was.

Half an hour later, though, as the full gloomy twilight of the arctic night closed around us, things were starting to look threatening. The wind was now a full gale, howling in the rigging; we were constantly lashed by spray as far back as the cockpit, and the lee or downwind rail was under green water most of the time.

Suddenly the cabin doors burst open and Tom's head appeared. He looked around him incredulously. 'What the fuck's going on here, you pair of clowns? What in hell's name are you trying to do... drown us all?' he yelled above the roar of water and wind.

'It's OK,' shouted Patrick. 'She's taking it in her stride...'

'It's bloody well not OK. We're putting a couple of reefs in right away. Everybody on deck, now!' Tom shouted down below. 'Safety lines, everybody, and Ros, can you take the wheel?' Ros had appeared in the cockpit and seemed to inhabit the space with a quiet authority I hadn't noticed before. 'Head her into wind; keep her as steady as you can,' Tom told her, before shouting, 'Patrick: sheet in the staysail and jib tight as they'll go. John: drop the mainsail, quick as you can now. Chris and Mike: furl the jib, right up, and don't forget to hang on to the furling line. Then everybody get ready to gather the sail and tie it tight, double reefing.'

As *Hirta* came round head to wind, all hell broke loose. The foresails flogged with a noise like thunder until Patrick sheeted them hard in. When you're straight into wind you catch the waves at an angle to the bow, so the boat yaws and rolls and pitches all at the same time. It's impossible to get a footing because of the waves, tonnes of green water breaking over the deck. It's hellish, and truly terrifying. You snap your safety line on to whatever solid thing you can, but more often than not it restricts your freedom of movement, so you unclip it and take the risk. And it is a risk. If you went over the side, you'd be gone for good. There would be no chance at all of finding you, let alone picking you up in this sort of sea, and you'd be frozen stiff in a matter of minutes, anyway.

Tom was unruffled; he gave orders with absolute coolness as he hauled the boom in amidships and kept an eye on every one of us. Ros, too, seemed to keep resolutely calm as she battled skilfully with the bucking wheel. As the sodden mainsail crashed down onto the boom, we all leaped to gather it and tie down the first reef. Each of a dozen ropes had to be passed beneath the sail and tied.

With the crazed rolling of the boat, the icy cold in your fingers, the difficulty of getting a purchase with your feet, and the cold, cold terror gnawing at your very innards, this is not an easy task. When we finally got the first reef tied, John dropped the sail a bit further and we set to tying in the second reef.

The whole job took about half an hour, then we hauled the now-much-reduced sail back up and tightened the outhauls. Tom cupped his hands over his mouth and yelled down the screaming wind: 'OK, Ros, pay her off the wind now and see how she sails like that.' Ros spun the wheel until the sails bellied out with wind and *Hirta* drove her bow into the boiling waves once more.

'Patrick,' said Tom, as we tumbled back into the shelter of the cockpit. 'Please don't ever do a thing like that again, not on my boat and not with a single member of my family and my crew on board.'

'Come on Tom, it wasn't that bad, and we both know the old girl was up to it well enough.' Patrick was bristling, but there was an element of sheepishness in his voice.

'This boat is a hundred years old, Patrick. She's well built and she's sound, but there's a limit, and you took her all the way to that limit. I shouldn't need to say this, but I'm the skipper and it's my responsibility to get you all safely to landfall. I cannot have you driving the boat on as if this were some sort of bloody military manoeuvre.'

Tom was furious, but he just about managed to rein himself in. The restraint was more intimidating than any outburst would have been.

'You're right, Tom,' said Patrick. 'I'm sorry. It won't happen again.'

AS IT WAS WELL INTO THE AFTER-MIDNIGHT WATCH, Patrick and I sloped off guiltily to our bunks for a couple of hours' sleep.

Sleep, or at least rest, is mandatory, as you need to be fit enough to take the next watch.

So I slumbered, listening fearfully to the storm that was still gathering strength. I was in my sleeping bag, wearing long-johns and T-shirt, with my moleskin trousers and heap of sodden jerseys at the foot of the bed and my oilskins hanging on a hook nearby. We'd each of us rigged up a lee cloth, a canvas strip tied to hooks above the berth, to stop ourselves getting hurled bodily from our beds.

As I lay there, thinking guiltily about Ana and the worries I'd so glibly dismissed, I was aware of John tumbling down the stairs and disappearing into the saloon to wake the skipper. A minute later Tom joined him by the chart table and I listened to them conferring. 'We can't carry on like this,' asserted John. 'The weather's still getting fiercer. If we don't put the third reef in a bit quick, we could lose the mast.'

I was already groping under my pillow for my glasses when Tom's shaggy mane poked into my berth. 'Get your butt up there on deck, Chris. Time for a third reef. Now!'

He went to wake Patrick while I rolled out of the berth, crawled into my oilskins and staggered up the pitching companionway steps straight from the warmth of my rank berth into the awfulness of a full gale on an arctic night.

'Right,' said Tom. 'You know what to do; do it. I'll take the wheel.'

The third and last reef was a little easier than the others, as there was less sail to deal with and fewer ties, although this was offset by the fact that the ferocity of the wind and the water was even more intense. We began like sleepwalkers, moving slowly, sleepily, but once smacked in the chops with a bucketful of icy green water you're back on the alert and moving fast.

Half an hour later Tom steered *Hirta* away from the wind to a point where she could just make headway through the now towering seas. 'I reckon that's a full storm; about force ten now,' he yelled above the din. 'Patrick and Chris, go and get some rest. Mike, go and make us some tea and we'll see if we can't make some sort of progress through this horror.'

Patrick and I crawled back below to our respective berths and attempted to salvage what little remained of our hours of rest – hard to do when distracted by the thought of a wall of grey water bursting asunder the cabin doors and drowning us like rats in a rabbit hutch, but exhaustion must have settled the matter.

In no time at all, I was shaken rudely awake by Mike. It was four in the morning.

'Hey, there's a storm out there and it's your turn to get out and in it,' he said with a nauseating grin.

'Is it getting any better?' I asked.

'Nope,' he answered, straight-faced this time. 'It's a whole lot worse.'

Getting into sopping, wet, icy clothes at four o'clock on a morning when you've been up most of the night is nobody's idea of fun. The violent motion of the boat made it an almost Herculean labour just to get a sock on. I asked myself if this really were the path to take in search of beauty... surely there must be less disagreeable ways.

I staggered out into a world of whirling greys. The sky was boiling down upon us in racing grey clouds; the sea was an unrelenting confusion of huge waves, each filling the air with its shattered crests of spray. John, drenched right through, gave me a wry grin from the wheel. 'We don't seem to be getting anywhere anyway, but see if you can't make due west, two seven zero.'

I wedged myself in beside the wheel, pulled my hat down over my glasses and appraised the situation. We were beating violently into a grey nothingness that whirled all about us. *Hirta* was sailing with just the staysail and a tiny patch of triple-reefed main. One minute the view was filled with nothing but a towering wall of grey water, and then we plunged into the trough and up the other side, to see nothing but the whirling grey tumult of the sky. Down in the troughs of the waves we would lose the wind, and the boat would momentarily right herself before being hurled aloft by the next wave, where the sails would again be taken by the wind and she would heel hard over once more. The motion was truly awful. And there was nothing to give a moment's comfort; not the sun nor the moon nor even the stars, nor the sight of a distant shore... just the crazed, if companionable, stares of the fulmars and storm petrels as they wheeled easily amongst the raging waves.

Things were getting so nasty that I decided to strap myself into the cockpit with the safety line. There was so much water breaking over the boat that I feared I might be swept away if a freak wave were to swamp us. It was a truly terrifying situation: we were three hundred miles from the nearest land, with no means of communication with any rescue services, and being tossed about like a feather in a whirlwind aboard a hundred-year-old sailing boat.

'This is nothing,' shouted Tom, who appeared beside me in the cockpit. 'It's nasty... very nasty... but this boat's been around for the best part of a century; she's been through a lot worse.'

'But what about you?' I hollered. 'Have you been in worse storms than this?'

'Many a time... and in less seaworthy boats; *Hirta* will see us through. Don't you worry about it.'

Tom's voice was reassuring but his face was set grim as he assessed the constantly changing situation and made the necessary decisions. For myself, I just wanted to avert my eyes from the awfulness of the tormented sea and sky around us. But I was on the helm and couldn't avoid looking at the sea. It had a mesmerising effect. The monstrousness of it made it seem unreal, although it was the real-est, coldest, wettest, most immediate and overpowering force I had ever faced.

And then I saw something I don't ever want to see again as long as I live: a colossal wall of dull grey water was bearing down on us. It obscured the very sky; it stood half as high as the mast. There was no way we could avoid being swamped. My legs went weak and I whimpered inwardly. 'Oh shit!' I cried (disappointing as last utterances go, I know, but there it is), and steeled myself for the crashing impact of a million merciless tonnes of seawater. At the same time I hauled on the wheel to steer into the wave. The bow rose, and *Hirta* seemed to look up like a tiny David confronting Goliath… and then… the monster just vanished. It rolled away beneath us. I looked behind as we surfed down the far side of it, and there it was, roaring away to the east. I almost wept with relief, and my heart welled with affection for the simple contrivance of hewn and shaped tree trunks that bore us safely across the fathomless abyss. *Hirta* had taken the wave in her stride. Our skipper was right.

He looked far from complacent, though, sitting solid and square in the corner of the cockpit, staring gravely at the storm. I watched him with one eye as I responded with the wheel to the dip and tug and roll of the boat each time she plunged into the trough of a wave or crashed over the crest. It was no longer a matter of steering a compass course; you just steered over each wave as it bore down upon the boat.

'What are you thinking, Tom?' I asked, when I couldn't stand the silence any more.

He bit his lip for a moment longer, then said, 'What I'm thinking is… we're not getting anywhere. There's too much wind, too heavy a sea, and it's all against us. It's taking hell out of the boat; taking hell out of all of us.'

He stopped to think a bit more, still chewing his lip.

'We have two options: we can turn and run before the storm, head back for Iceland...'

'Or...?' I asked.

'Or... or we heave to, batten down the hatches and just ride the storm out. It's a couple of crap options, but there you go. We'll put it to the vote.'

IN THE EVENT, nobody wanted to run back to Iceland, abandoning all the westerly progress we had already made. Nobody much fancied heaving to, either, but it seemed the better option, so that's what we did.

Looking back on it, it seems almost beyond belief that we would just have stopped right out there in the middle of the North Atlantic, stopped dead, rocking about day after day in our infinitesimal speck of a boat. There we were, suspended in tumult somewhere between the moon and the core of the earth, seven minuscule humans, tossed like a walnut in a millrace, waiting, just waiting, for the anger of the storm to pass.

To prepare for heaving to, we lashed the wheel to starboard and pulled the two sails in so they were angled to channel the winds safely, like sheep through a pen. The result was that the wind steadied the boat while driving us very slowly sideways back where we had come from.

One man would be on watch at all times, tied into the cockpit. One-hour watches; after that you'd be frozen half to death, to say nothing of being frightened out of your wits. Down below we did what we could to adopt some semblance of normal human existence; not all that easy when you've six people tumbling around in the confines of a tiny wooden cabin. I wondered at the infinite capacity of human beings to adapt.

Ros, strapped tightly into the galley, cooked meals, wonderful meals of mutton and bacon and beans. The cooker, like all the oil lamps in the cabin, was on gimbals – an ingenious system of pivots which meant that it stayed horizontal no matter what the angle of the boat; otherwise the pans would have been constantly slopping their hot contents all over the cook. The cabin table was fitted with a fiddle, a raised wooden surround, which, with the aid of some miraculously sticky place mats, prevented the plates flying off the table into the laps of first the diners on one side, then on the other.

We adopted strategies for dealing with everything: you timed your lunge from galley to table with your plate of stew, to the pitching of the boat. The pitching was more or less predictable, so in one lunge you could get to the bulkhead at the end of the chart table. There you wedged yourself in tight, holding the stew aloft, while the boat toppled crazily over the other way; then, as she started to come over again, you made the final dive and at the bottom of the roll slumped neatly down onto the seat and waited for the next roll to slap your stew down on the non-slip mat. Thus seven people fed three times a day.

When we weren't eating, we would read... some would have their heads deep in the Vinland sagas, or some earnest nautical tome. I myself found it impossible to concentrate on anything more complex than Edward Lear and so, at Hannah's insistence, reverted to reciting 'The Jumblies'. Oddly enough, I derived the greatest comfort from joining her in declaiming:

And when the Sieve turned round and round
And every one cried, 'You'll all be drowned!'
They called aloud, 'Our Sieve ain't big,
But we don't care a button! We don't care a fig!
In a Sieve we'll go to sea!'

We may have been in the middle of a nightmare, but that didn't mean we were without pleasures; after all, you can only be catatonic with fright for a certain limited period. When the source of the fear is with you night and day, roaring and whirling just an oaken hull away from you and your dinner, your fear – and I make no bones about admitting that I was absolutely terrified – soon takes second place to other, gentler things: conversation, laughter, reading, hope, the minutiae of daily existence. Also there was the inspiring example of little Hannah, who seemed hardly perturbed at all. She had adapted immediately, in the way that children will, to her new environment. Ros and Tom would read to her and play, just as if they were at home in their cosy cottage in the New Forest, and she was happy.

There was an odd sort of cosiness about the situation, too. The saloon was lit by oil lamps, which cast the most romantic glow, and a comforting warmth came from the little pot-bellied stove in the corner. Everywhere you looked there was some big lug of a man sprawled out like a dog, reading a book or dozing, rocking involuntarily with the motion of the boat. And there was a heavy and complex odour about the place, composed of diesel, meat stew, the fishy smell of the sea, outbreaks of flatulence, and the putrid miasma of unwashed bodies and wet wool. This was far from pleasant, but you can get to like anything with familiarity. As I said, it was oddly cosy.

BY COMMON CONSENT, even when things were as bad as they were now, we the men would go on deck to take a leak. The heads could become unpleasantly congested with the daily traffic of five men, so they were reserved for what you might call sit-down occasions, and for the more refined use of Hannah and Ros.

Now, as you may imagine, it was far from pleasant going up onto the storm-lashed deck to relieve yourself, so you would try and hold things in until it was your watch, when you had to go on deck anyway. This was not always possible, though. You might, for instance, be in your berth, thinking ruefully of your loved ones and the home you suspected you might not get to see again, and little by little that familiar old insistent urge would steal over you. It might be one o'clock in the morning, and you're not on watch till four. You wonder if perhaps you could hold it back... for three hours? No, impossible. You lie back and try to forget it... Maybe it'll go away. You try to think of something different, but to no avail.

And so, wearily, you set the long tedious process in motion: first you unzip your sleeping bag, whereupon most of that lovely warmth you have worked so hard to create vanishes. Then you wriggle out of its clinging silken folds and the tangle of the woollen inner. Next you reach up in the dark to untie the lee cloth, grateful that you were sensible enough to tie it properly with a couple of bows, because little by little the urge is getting stronger upon you now. With the lee cloth down, you have a little more freedom of movement, so you reach down and, with an unimaginable contortion, take hold of your sopping-wet moleskin trousers and fight your way into them, still supine and in the dark. By the time you fasten the zip you are exhausted, so you lie back for a moment and groan quietly to yourself.

Now it's time to roll out of the berth and wedge yourself into the dark passage, while you scrabble about for the three or four layers of upper woollens that are essential if you're not going to freeze up solid the moment you emerge from the cabin. This takes a long time, because the sweaters are partly inside out and partly the right way round, and they're wet and mouldering, and also because while this is going on you are being hurled back and forth like a fish in a washing machine.

Now to select your boots from the heap haphazardly tumbled by the companionway steps. You squeeze your feet into them, only to find that you have left a pair of thick sopping-wet socks scrunched up in the bottom. By this time you are so desperate for relief that you can't think straight, so you put on somebody else's boots... but you're not there yet. No, not by a long chalk.

Oilskins are next, and getting into oilskin trousers with your boots already on is hard enough in bright daylight on dry land. You wonder if maybe you ought to take the boots off and put the trousers on without the boots, but then you remember that the trousers must be outside the boots or else your boots will be full of seawater within five seconds of going outside.

Braces over the shoulders, and on with the oilskin jacket; button it up and zip it to keep the wind and waves out. Spectacles next, a quick swipe to clean them, woollen hat and finally wet wool gloves and you're ready, and not before time, as your bladder's on the point of exploding. You grasp the companionway rail and climb the first step... Oh-oh... what about your safety line? Back down into the cabin, untangle it from all the others on the same hook, slip it over your shoulders, clip it together at the front and scuttle back down the passage and up the ladder.

You burst through the doors. The icy blast almost knocks the breath from your body. There's Mike lashed into the cockpit, salt spray streaming down his glasses, his mouth open like a dying cod. He wants to talk because he's been sitting there like that for the last hour with nothing but the wind and the waves for company.

You ignore him and with an oath and a grunt... because things are getting beyond a joke now... you scramble out of the cockpit and head as best you can for the lee shrouds.

Bugger the safety line; you've got to get there fast now. You slip as a wave bursts over the bow, bark your shin on the cabin skylight and roll down into the scuppers beneath the rail. That's OK, it's more or less where you need to be, anyway. Grabbing the shroud, you haul yourself to your feet and snap the safety line onto it.

Now I know that there will be those who may find this indelicate, but I feel constrained to relate here a particular difficulty that flings itself in the path of this most natural bodily function. The sensitive reader might prefer to skip a page or two and join us later on the trip, as there are details which I feel must be chronicled.

So there you are, shackled safely to the lee shrouds, up to your knees in raging green water. The lee side, you see, being downwind, is more often than not completely under water. (One of the first lessons you learn when you start sailing is – for reasons that are pretty obvious – not to pee off the windward side of a boat.)

Now at this point there's a terrible danger that you might momentarily lose the urge and decide that you don't actually want to take a leak after all and that you might as well just return to your cabin. But it's a delusion and you delay at your peril. Luckily you are wise to this; it has happened too many times before. You remove your gloves; you cannot under any circumstances take a piss with gloves on. This is easy enough, although, despite the fact that you have shackled the safety line to the shroud, you still have to hold on with one hand or else you'd be in and out of the water like a yoyo. Next, fumble for the buttons and the zip on the oilskin bottoms... not easy with your one free hand, but after a little inept fiddling about you manage to get it open.

Mike is watching you from the cockpit with steadily increasing interest – he's that bored.

Now for the moleskins. Mine, interestingly enough, belonged to the explorer Sir Ranulph Fiennes, and have the name 'Ran' written in Biro on the waistband. He wore these trousers on his Arctic and Antarctic adventure, and sold them off at Camden Lock along with a whole rake of other stuff from the expedition. That's where I got the fancy sleeping bag, too. But the moleskin trousers are by far my favourite possession – a reminder that we are all, in our own small way, fellow explorers.

They also have a very fine weatherproof zip, which, with frozen fingers, requires a lot of fumbling to get undone... but somehow eventually you do. That's two layers; two more to go. Long johns, or the particular type that I was wearing, have a small aperture covered by a sort of pocket. You manage to insert a couple of questing fingers as you peer downwards to see if you can see anything, which of course you can't, because your glasses are soaked in salt spray and it's almost dark and, besides, there's not that much to see anyway; these things are best done by feel.

This, of course, is where your problems begin. You search in the gap between this opening and the top of your inside underpants with increasing but unavailing desperation. Can you locate the organ in question? Can you hell! You're being buffeted back and forth like a shuttlecock, it's freezing cold and you're scared half to death. A glance back at the cockpit confirms your suspicion that you're still being watched by Mike. If anything he's staring more intently.

Now here I should remind our readers that the male of the species is prone to a certain... shall we say reticence, and indeed shrinkage, in circumstances of extreme stress. An involuntary survival mechanism kicks in to protect that which we hold dear until a less inopportune moment should present itself. You look round, startled by a shout from the cockpit. It's the unspeakable Mike.

'What's the matter, then?' he shouts. 'Can't find your dick?' He then convulses with fatuous laughter at his own crass joke.

Your desperation increases, if that's possible. There's just got to be a penis in there somewhere, surely... it was there the last time you came on deck.

After long, long minutes of ineffectual fumbling, your search may be rewarded, but even then it's no simple matter to coax the poor thing out through the long threatening sphincter of elastic and wool and buttons and zips. But then finally you get there, and you hang in the shrouds directing the long steaming arc into the frozen grey wastes of the north Atlantic... oh, the sweet and blessed relief. And now back to bed.

FOR THREE DAYS and three long nights we lay buffeted by the elements at some point between Iceland and Greenland. We kept up our routine of an hour on watch, then back to the cabin, though to be honest it probably made no difference if anyone were at the wheel or not. Indeed, when any of us were woken for our watch – perhaps by John, his beard dripping icy water into the cup of tea that he'd brought – there would always be a few minutes, struggling with the pantomine of putting on foul weather clothes, while *Hirta* bucked and plunged, alone and unwatched, with us seven vulnerable souls shut below.

Still, we took our watches seriously. First I would go forward and, shackling myself to the forestay, scan what I could see of the horizon. Nothing, just grey heaving sea in all directions, populated sparsely by the odd baffled-looking fulmar. Next I would check that all the lashings and stays were tight, that everything was in place. And finally I would return to the cockpit, strap myself in, and busy myself with watching the waves as they burst over the bow and come sweeping knee-deep along the deck to pour out of the scuppers. It was raining hard, too, although even heavy rain didn't make that much difference because we were already lashed by the salt spray that flew from the wave tops.

I would pull the peak of my woollen ferreting cap down over my glasses and hug myself against the cold. Wedged into the cockpit by the wheel at the back of the boat was one of the best places to be; the weight of the engine was at the back, so that's the most stable part, and from a relatively still platform I could watch the bow with its long bowsprit rearing into the sky only to crash back among the waves, each time in a hissing cloud of spray that scattered instantly on the wind. You can scarcely imagine a thing so dramatic and beautiful. I recalled being on holiday at Trebarwith Strand in Cornwall, aged ten, as a storm came roaring in from the west and gave the most dazzling performance on the rocks. I sat there for what seemed like hours watching the beating of the monstrous waves against the rocks, eating a '99' cornet, if I remember right.

We had almost got used to storm life onboard when, round about the middle of the morning on the fourth day, there came a lightening in the unrelenting greys of our world. A cloud-like smoke whirled away for a moment, and behind it a brief glimpse of the palest disc and, looking down, a hint of a glitter and a shine in the joyless matt grey of the waves. Within an hour we were down to a fierce gale, but seemingly a wild thing of exuberance, crying exultantly farewell as it hurtled away to the east.

Four hours later and the sea itself was settling; the wind moderated and veered a little, so we shook out a reef and bounded again towards the west. There was a tangible sense of relief to be sailing again: everybody laughed easily and the old refrains and jokes were taken out again and dusted off. Patrick and Tom sat down and thrashed out their differences in the matter of boat handling and came to a perfectly sensible agreement. Meanwhile the rest of us had returned to the Jumblies:

And every one said, 'If we only live,
We too will go to sea in a Sieve—
To the hills of the Chankly Bore!'

As our course took us northwest towards the southern tip of Greenland, the ice cap, the greatest repository of frozen fresh water on the planet, the very air began to freeze. We had thought it was cold before but this was different, and we felt it. And we already had all our cold-weather gear on, so there was nothing left to add.

Day after day we scudded on towards the west, sometimes chugging along with the engine, sometimes driven like a leaf before a gale, and at others, more rarely, gliding across the shining swell with the wind behind us. This was a lovely motion that tended, with its feeling of being lifted and gently hurled forwards to where we wanted to go, to induce in us all a mild euphoria. Sometimes the clouds lifted a little and then there was an intense, crystalline brightness to the air and the sea. The sea would turn glassy all around, not a ship not a boat; nobody else was crazy enough to be out and up at these sort of latitudes. All the more sensible sailors were cruising across the milder bluer seas of the world: the Mediterranean and the Caribbean.

On one of those glassy days, I was leaning on the shrouds, staring idly around, when I noticed the slightest puckering of the surface away in the distance... then nothing. I must have imagined it... but then again, a little more and closer. Patrick noticed it too. Soon it was unmistakeable. Dolphins. There were scores of them, and they came racing playfully from the distant horizon towards our boat, leaping like puppies and dancing and diving as they came. I had never seen dolphins before and I was unprepared, so far out in the loveless wastes of the northern ocean, for such a dazzling display of physical exuberance.

They gathered round the boat and rolled and dived beneath the hull; they weaved joyously amongst one another as they hurtled along riding the bow wave, now diving deep, now leaping full clear of the water. A little ahead and to one side a dolphin leaped right out of the water and with muscular thrusts of its tail, performed two or three skips across the surface before falling with a great splosh back beneath the waves. They didn't tire of their games; they played and played, on and on... and we too were almost leaping with excitement on the deck. Hannah squealed with utter delight. But we were all swept up in the same astonished thrill. I climbed the mast and from high above the deck watched their glorious antics. The water was clear and I could see their great dark glistening bodies way below us, spiralling up and twisting over to show their pale undersides.

You couldn't help but be foolish and imagine that those tiny eyes of theirs, deep in their protective hoods of blubber, were smiling and laughing at the sheer fun of it. I had seen a similar phenomenon with a flock of crag martins, forty or so of them horsing around in the sunshine and shade of the rocks by the shore in Greece. The only explanation I could possibly think of for this behaviour was that it was a manifestation of sheer animal joy. Me, I found myself whooping with pleasure. All the cold and the boredom and the misery and the fear of the journey were amply repaid by such a sight.

The others were a little dewy-eyed about the dolphins, too, for although every long-distance sailor has often seen them, it's a sight you don't tire of. And from here on, as we crossed the Greenland Sea, there were dolphins with us almost all the time, and we felt comforted by the presence of such benignity. Until now we had had fulmars and skuas and cormorants and gannets; creatures that had both moved and fascinated us, and kept us company in times and places of loneliness and fear. For this I'd felt a certain gratitude and respect. But the dolphins... well, the dolphins are mammals; they are 'one of us'.

We had been hoping to make a landfall on the coast of Greenland but the ice reports had not painted a rosy picture of the seaways up to those ports: there was pack ice and drifting ice and the westerlies had blown all the ice from the west side of the Sea of Labrador over to the east, where it was blocking access to the coast. This, of course, was back in the 1980s; if you'd a mind to today, you could sail round the Greenland coast in your Cornish Crabber. There's almost no sea ice left.

'Trouble is,' said Tom, 'that you can be sailing in the evening through waters lightly packed with thin sheets of ice that just tickle the sides of the boat as she passes, and then you wake up in the morning and it's turned to slabs of pack ice six feet thick. That's the way it is up in these beastly latitudes. Give me the Torrible Zone any day... and the hills of the Chankly Bore.'

So we didn't make Greenland – it was just too damn dangerous in a wooden boat – although that evening we passed close enough to the southern tip to be able to make out, in the faintest of pastel blues, Cape Farewell. We watched it wistfully for an hour or two as we passed, and warmed our bellies with whisky.

The next day there was mist in the morning, and something new to talk about: John had spotted a growler.

'So tell me about your growler,' I suggested as I emerged on deck.

'You can see for yourself,' said John. 'There it is, right behind us.'

I looked back to where he was pointing. There it was, a rather unexciting block of white ice bobbing about on the sea.

'It doesn't look much to me,' I said, a little disparagingly.

'It may not look much to you, Chris,' said Tom. 'But if we'd hit it at the speed we were going, it would have stoved in the front of the boat, and we wouldn't have been here now, nicely up on the surface of the sea; we'd have been well on our way down below it. From now on, this being growler country – and maybe there'll even be icebergs, too – we're having a man on the bow on lookout day and night. So off you go and wipe the breakfast out of your beard and then get shackled onto the forestay; it's your turn first.'

Keeping watch on the forestay was different from being in the cockpit. There was no shelter for a start; you were right out there on the front of the boat, peering keenly into the mist. You had to see the growlers and bergs; it was simply a question of life and death. This made me feel very important, and feeling important kept me good and alert for at least fifteen minutes. But then the intense cold and the tedium of the thing began to kick in. There didn't seem to be any more growlers in this particular patch of sea. I turned round and grinned at Patrick, who was at the helm. He waved back. Then I jumped up and down a bit, to see if I couldn't get some circulation going again. Next I leaned my back against the forestay and recited the whole of 'The Dong with the Luminous Nose', then I did 'The Jumblies'. And then I saw the growler.

It was a hundred yards away off the port bow, so it didn't pose any threat to us. 'Growler off the port bow, Pat,' I said in a seamanlike way, mainly in order to give the impression that I was alert and doing my job. We watched it as it bobbed away into the mist. That's what growlers do: they move with the waves, in contrast to an iceberg, which sits four square and serene. Growlers are chips off icebergs or broken bits of pack ice that have fled south on the winds and tides. They tend to be somewhere between the size of a small room and a big house and they get scattered all over the northern oceans. Of course, to a great ship of iron and steel they barely represent a hazard, but to a small wooden boat like ours a collision with a growler would mean the end of the line.

I resumed my watch; there was nothing to see as we butted on through the mist. I stared and stared as hard as I could, and soon there seemed to be wraiths and plumes of swirling cloud in the enfolding whiteness, and then shadows of grey which might be the walls of soaring icebergs just ahead, or more likely just the play of the breeze in the mist. I looked down into the bow wave to reset my vision. I looked up and there was a growler dead ahead.

'GROWLERDEADAHEADPAT!!' I yelled. 'HARD A STARBOARD NOW!'

Patrick swung the wheel hard over and the growler slipped along the port side. It glowed and gleamed in purest white and turquoise and froze the very air around it. Patrick spun the helm back and the sails took up the wind once more.

'Blimey, that was a close one,' I said, as I wiped the mist from my glasses. 'I think it's your turn up on the front now, Pat. I'm about frozen solid.'

'You've another fifteen minutes, by my reckoning.'

I grumbled quietly and wrapped myself tightly round the forestay, peering still into the mist. There was something out there, something enormous.

'WHAT IN THE NAME OF HEAVEN IS THAT, PAT?' I shouted.

'What, where?'

'That bloody great thing lying on the water over there, look at it!'

'Holy mother of God, it's a whale. It's a bloody great whale!'

Patrick stood up and looked at the apparition openmouthed, then shouted down the companionway: 'Whale ahoy!' Then he felt a little self-conscious about what he'd just shouted and said, 'There's a whale up here, lads, come and have a look,' but this time more quietly.

Now, the whale was not like the dolphins; it wasn't horsing about, it was much quieter, more dignified. Then it blew, a great wet whoomph from its blowhole, and over all the Labrador Sea there spread a great miasma of marine flatulence, a thing with overtones of krill and plankton and seaweed and whole hosts of the fishy animalcules of the northern oceans.

By now everybody was sitting on deck in awed silence. It was as if we had just seen God.

'Pooh,' said Hannah, pinching her nose, then thought better of it and joined in the awe.

The great creature swished its flukes idly and drifted through the water, easily keeping pace with us. It was bigger even than the boat, probably sixty feet or more. It was a finback, one of the most enormous creatures on the planet. There we were drifting in perfect silence alongside one of the few remaining survivors of the great whales, for man has pursued and hunted these peaceful creatures to the very verge of extinction. I had seen film of the appalling things we do to whales, of the pilot whale cull in the Faroe Islands, where they corral hundreds of these small whales into a shallow bay, using motorboats and nets. Then, when the poor confused creatures find themselves in water too shallow to manoeuvre, they are set upon and butchered by scores of men wielding axes and flensing hooks. The sea runs literally red with their blood. And this is done not as a matter of survival, nor of necessity, but as a ritual for men to prove their manhood.

Two hundred years of whaling doesn't seem to have convinced whales of the evil intentions of men and they have retained their peacefulness and their curiosity. For a long time our finback kept station with the boat, as if it were interested in us. Then eventually it sounded again and dived, leaving us with a flourish of its colossal flukes, shiny, barnacled and running with seawater.

NIGHT BEGAN TO FALL as we ran towards the coast of Newfoundland, a deeper, darker night than we had been used to, for the summer was drawing on and we were a lot farther south now. Once again the port and starboard lamps glowed red and green against the mainsail. The wind had come round behind us at last, and we were loping along in great bounds across a long lazy swell. There was a mood of high anticipation onboard, as after nineteen days at sea it looked like we might at last see land.

Tom was on deck, staring ahead into the falling darkness; I was at the helm with Patrick perched out on the bow. There was still a risk of the occasional growler, and we had recently picked up a signal on our radio direction finder, a series of four beeps followed by a silence, like the flashes and occlusions of a lighthouse. The pattern told us that the beacon was on the coast of northern Newfoundland. Unfortunately, because we couldn't get another signal, we had no way of establishing exactly how far we were from the coast. We knew the line down which we were sailing to reach the coast, but had no idea of where we were on it. We hadn't had a reliable sun sight for several days because we had been sailing through mists, probably caused by warm air currents colliding with cold air currents or some such thing.

Anyway, Tom didn't like it.

'We're running down onto a lee shore with a big wind up our arse, night falling fast and no way of knowing how far off we are. It's a classic recipe for disaster. No one's going to like this, but I'm afraid we're going to have to turn around and head back the way we've come.'

We looked gloomily into the rushing dark. So near and yet so far. We had all been looking forward so much to the land. On land there were women and there was beer and bars, and flowers and trees and a certain undeniable solidity to things, which was conspicuously lacking at sea. We all wanted it… and we wanted it tonight.

'Pat,' called Tom to the shadowy figure hanging from the forestay. 'I think we're going to have to beat back out to sea. What do you reckon?'

'Well, I tell you what, skipper: I think you'd be crazy to keep running in towards this coast in the dark. I may be hallucinating out here on the bow, but I keep thinking I can hear the sound of waves crashing onto rocks. We could be fifty miles off… but we could be no more than half a mile away.'

'OK, Chris,' ordered Tom. 'Bring her about. Pat, you come back here and haul in the foresail sheets.'

I swung the wheel and the boat described a great curve away from the longed-for land. Tom hauled in the yards and yards of mainsheet and we resumed our more usual motion of beating hard into an oncoming sea.

And so all the long dark hours of that night we fled from the land, for if there's anything more terrifying than the fathomless depths of the ocean – and, let's face it, they're pretty terrifying – then it's the hungry rocks of the land. If worldwide there is a big ship lost at sea once a week (for that is the figure), then the figure for ships wrecked on the rocks must be many times that.

At dawn, however, we turned again and ran towards the south. I was asleep when the lookout spied the land, at first the faintest of blue lines on the southern horizon, and by the time I came on deck there was a distinct line of low, green hills. It was still a long way off but we could already smell it. I had thought this was the most fanciful of notions – the belief that sailors can smell the land long before they see it – but take it from me, you can. We were all on deck in the early morning, bundled up against the cold and sniffing the air like a pack of dogs. I could smell flowers (which is what you're supposed to be able to smell), and I could also smell bread and women, and cakes and hay. It seemed extraordinary, and I wondered about it for a bit, and came to the conclusion that we were closing with an entire continent, and that from Halifax to Vancouver there were countless bakers baking bread and cakes, and millions of women scented and powdered, and prairies of new-mown hay drying in the August sunshine. All these scents were rising on the cushion of warm air above the land and falling to earth over the cooler sea, where they drove mariners insane with longing for the loveliness of the land.

THE NEW WORLD

NOW, THE IMPORTANT THING when you make a landfall is that your boat looks good. The wind and the tides were on our side and we were able to make our approach into the bay of Quirpon all standing, which means with all the sails up and looking pretty damn good for the benefit of any nautical-minded folk who might be watching. At the last minute we rounded up, dropped the bags and, with the skipper standing proud at the wheel, edged in to the long wooden jetty. Mike sprang across the narrowing gap with the head rope; I took the stern line and we made fast to a couple of bollards.

Then we climbed back onboard and joined in the general preparations for going ashore. This meant folding the sails tight and neat in a 'harbour stow', flaking down all the ropes and lines and generally tidying up the boat. Then we washed and shaved in salt water from buckets on the deck, and finally dressed ourselves in clean, dry finery for that great moment when we would march along the dock and greet the natives. It was pretty exciting for Mike and me, as neither of us had set foot on the soil of the New World before, and we were unsure what to expect.

On the jetty were a number of men all dressed more or less alike in dungarees, thick check shirts and baseball caps. They were bent intently over what they were doing... mending nets, I shouldn't wonder, as it's fishing that makes things tick around these parts. Not one of them so much as raised his head at our arrival; to our surprise, and indeed chagrin, they took not the slightest bit of notice. It was hard to believe: you'd have thought that the arrival out of the northeast of a boat that looked like something out of a romantic historical drama, with all her sails set and flags flying, would have excited a certain interest. But no – these were the most phlegmatic of men.

'Right,' said Tom. 'I guess we'd better go and make ourselves known to these good people.'

We all climbed over the rail and onto the dock. Together we took two swaggering strides and promptly keeled right over... all of us in a chaotic and undignified heap. At this, one or two of the fishermen almost imperceptibly raised their heads and mumbled something with the faintest play of a smile. We picked ourselves up and, with circumspection and intense concentration, stumbled on. You get your sea legs, but when you've been at sea for days on end you lose your land legs, and so our first longed-for taste of terra firma was letting us down; the land was rolling and lurching, so it seemed, all over the place.

Tom staggered towards one of the fishermen. 'Good morning to you. We've just come from Iceland…' He left a pause for the enormity of this statement to sink in.

The man looked with great deliberation up at him from beneath the peak of his baseball cap, while we wobbled about on the dock behind our skipper. Eventually, after perhaps a minute, he said: 'Iceland, huh? I guess that's a mighty long way off.'

We were clearly in a land where words and ideas were accorded their full due dignity; snappy badinage was not what these people did.

'Yup,' continued Tom. 'Nineteen days and headwinds all the way.' Behind Tom we simpered modestly as one, but this statement failed to elicit a response. Then the man rose to his feet and held out his hand.

'Y'all welcome to Quirpon,' he enunciated.

Wobbling still, but wreathed in grins of jolly bonhomie, we clambered over one another in our eagerness to shake our fisherman's hand. This was a big moment.

Tom continued: 'I guess we'd better report our arrival to customs and immigration.'

Our man mulled this over for a bit, while we busied ourselves looking around at what we could see of Quirpon. It didn't look like the sort of place that would have a customs and immigration: there was the jetty and a few sheds of a lowly sort, and a clapboard shack or two. In confirmation of which, our new friend said: 'Ain't no customs and 'magrayshun in Quirpon.' Then, by way of explanation: 'Jus' too darn small.'

'What do you suppose we should do, then?' asked Tom.

'There's Wally Stocks down in Griguet; he's a customs man. Maybe y'all should see him.'

'And how would we get to Griguet?' (pronounced 'grigget').

'Guess I'll take y'all there in the pickup.'

And so we found ourselves speeding down the gravel road to Griguet – Tom, Ros and Hannah in the cab with our new friend, who was called Eli Bridger, the rest of us heaped happily in the open back.

Later that afternoon we had tea with the Bridgers. Eli and his family lived in a little wooden house on the rocks on the edge of the bay of Griguet. From the kitchen where we sat warm as toast by the wood-fired cooking range, we could see the beautiful bay, shining blue, the surface unruffled, sheltered by the horns of low-lying land that almost met at the entrance.

Eli's wife was called Lee-Anne and she was as talkative as he was taciturn. Her speciality was baking and there we were all sat laying waste a huge plate of fairy cakes she had baked that afternoon. Ros and Hannah, who were more fastidious about these things than the rest of us, were taking a long, hot shower. The kitchen, smelling of tea and cakes and a hint of woodsmoke, was the sweetest cosiest thing after the trackless wastes of the north Atlantic.

Later, sated with cake and awash with strong tea, I turned again to gaze at the beauty of the bay. To my horror it had completely disappeared. Where before there had been a glorious sheet of calm water, now I was looking at what looked like a scrapyard full of decomposing pickup trucks, rusty engine blocks and heaps of assorted junk. It was hideous. What in the name of heaven had happened while I had been drinking my tea?

It transpired that the tide had gone out to reveal the arrangements made by the locals for mooring their boats. The custom was that, when your pickup truck died, you ran it into the bay at low tide and there, with a stout chain passed through the windows, it served as a mooring block for your boat. It was hard not to admire the good sense of it.

There's not a great deal happens in Griguet, so, in contrast to our first impressions, our arrival caused quite a stir. We were adopted by the Bridgers, who were as generous and kind as folks can possibly be, and I suppose got a certain amount of kudos from the fact that we were always round at their place. They took us to Lanso Meadows – or L'Anse aux Méduses – where the Vikings, whose journey we had been following, had made their first settlement. There was a museum and the reconstruction of some of the turf-roofed longhouses. It was a bleak, wind-blasted spot, open to the ocean to the north, but I suppose that, to the Vikings, after many weeks tossed by storms across the sea in an open boat, even a settlement as comfortless as L'Anse aux Méduses would have seemed as cosy as Lee-Anne Bridger's kitchen.

It was an odd thought, that this was the first settlement on the New World by Europeans, five hundred years before Cabot or Columbus made their more lasting marks. We all cast about for meaningful observations on this singular truth, which is complicated by the fact that when John Cabot arrived in 1497 to claim the New World for the British Crown, there were no fewer than a thousand Basque fishermen already there, drying the cod they had caught on the Grand Banks. This must have taken the wind from his sails somewhat.

WALKING ALONG THE QUAYSIDE, distracted a little by the sharp angles of pickup trucks poking out of the water, Eli and his son Jeb told us about the cod fishing. There had been a time when it was said that a man could walk across the Grand Banks on the backs of the cod; for hundreds of years it had been the greatest fishery in the world. But the size of the catches, and the size of the fish, had dwindled to almost nothing, and it was the same story with the smaller inland fisheries like this one. It was no longer possible to make a living from fishing, especially as the sea here was frozen solid in the winter months.

'Yup,' said Jeb. 'Whole darn sea's frozen solid just as far as you can see. You can make a hole and take a fish or two for the family, but there ain't no money in it.'

'So how do you make a living?' I asked. It was something I'd been wondering about for a while.

'Well, there's only one way hereabouts. We take some seals. It's all there is in the winter.'

'Seals?' There was a pause.

'Yup, seals,' repeated Jeb a little less certainly.

'What do you mean?' asked John.

'We cull 'em,' said Jeb. 'We jus' take the young 'uns. The furriers pay well for the pelt.'

'You mean you're... seal clubbers?'

'Well, that's sure the way we kill 'em: quick crack on the head with a club. Kills 'em instantly.'

These were our new friends – the very acme of kindness and generosity – and we struggled to take this revelation on board. A pall of silence descended as Jeb went on to explain his work.

'What you gotta remember', he told us, 'is that there's millions and millions o' them seals out there. On the coast of Labrador just across the water, there's a colony with about four million seals. It ain't just man who's overfishing the cod; it's them darn seals, too. If we go out of a morning and so much as see a single seal, we turn right about and come home again. You'll never catch a fish when there's seals about. So they gotta be culled.'

'But what about the clubbing?' I held out.

'Be a whole lot easier to shoot 'em with a rifle, but it don't do the job quick enough, so we ain't allowed to use rifles. The club kills 'em right away. It ain't a nice thing to have to do, but then nor's killin' fish... an' not cows nor pigs nor lambs, neither.'

We listened quietly, gazing at our respective feet or the distant horizon, as Jeb tried to put the facts straight.

'I tell you the controls is strict, too. You gotta have a licence and there's fishery protection officers there all the time. There's any irregularity, you lose your licence, and there ain't nobody here can afford to do that.'

A COUPLE OF DAYS LATER I WATCHED as Hirta hoisted her sails and tacked out of the harbour to start her run down the eastern seaboard. She was laden to the gunwales with fairy cakes, dried fish and the warmth and good wishes of the Bridgers of Griguet. For a long time I stood on the dock and waved. It was such a lovely sight, I couldn't leave until she had disappeared from view behind the hills to the east. Then I gathered up my pack and my guitar, and headed off to see the New World... or at least Newfoundland and Nova Scotia. I wanted a spell on land, and a little independence, so I had forged a plan to hitch down through Newfoundland, across to Nova Scotia, and meet up with the boat in a week's time in Lunenburg.

I trudged off down the cinder track that led south out of Quirpon. You can walk a long way among the blueberries and the cloudberries in northern Newfoundland before you get a lift. And so I spent a glorious seven days alone and on the solid unmoving road, wandering slow and easy down from the north. I walked for hour after hour, dreaming of home a little and longing for love. Sometimes people took me in, other nights I slept in barns or cheap hotels in the towns. And I ate lobster for the first time, when I got a lift with a lobster fisherman.

'Man, you never ate a lobster?' he questioned me in amazement. 'Why, we'll have one right away. I got a whole heap of 'em in back of the truck.' And there, on a warm late summer afternoon by the clear water of the Bras d'Or lakes, he persuaded a reluctant lobster to get into the cooking pot, and together we dismembered it with our pocket knives and devoured its sweet pink flesh.

I arrived in Lunenburg before *Hirta* did, and checked into a white wooden hotel just behind the waterfront. I was the only guest in the place and it wasn't very big anyway, so I had the undivided attention of the beautiful Martha, who ran the place and exuded such a welcome aura of warm femininity and subtle scent that it quite befuddled my brain. It was then that I fell prey to homesickness; it came in waves, coloured with tender thoughts of Ana. I didn't know how long I would have to wait for the boat, so I decided to channel my seething emotions into art. I bought a sketchbook and set about immortalising the pretty little town in ink and wash.

In the morning I would wander out to the rocks on the point and eagerly scan the sea for the sight of a red sail. Later I would walk on the hills around the town, sit in the street and sketch or play some guitar, until I could wander back for dinner. Ah, dinner... I sat alone in the dining room with a candle on my table, freshly picked flowers and a bottle of wine, and I swear I have never eaten such food. It was mostly the vegetables, the crisp pungent flavour of them, and their moist and glistening hues, but when the dessert arrived, creations of succulent berries gloriously enhanced by the products of the dairy cow and the humble hen, well, I was almost in heaven.

Perhaps Hirta would never come, and I would spend the rest of my days, sitting on the point watching for a sail, munching on exquisite vegetables. Half a week passed and I became fretful, wandering out at first light to scan the horizon or distractedly penning portraits of the boat in small heroic sketches.

Then at last, in the late afternoon light, *Hirta* appeared, cutting through the bay with all sails billowing, gleaming crimson in the low rays of the sun. I watched, entranced as she tacked in a graceful extended zigzag towards the harbour. They knew I would be watching from somewhere, so they were putting on a show, and I wasn't disappointed. I was so excited to see them again that I jumped up and down and hooted and hollered from the cliffs, but it was too far off, so I ran down to the dock, arriving just in time to take the lines.

How strange they looked, my shipmates. We had been used to one another huge and amorphous, swaddled in layer upon layer of woollens, topped by shiny oilskins. But now we had been slipping down the lines of latitude towards the warmth of late summer, and bit by bit we had shed our protective clothing, revealing ourselves as less substantial beings. We had become etiolated, too, like plants growing beneath stones, denied the light and warmth of the sun. The skin that was on display shone in mottled shades of white and pink, with here and there a dash of livid red from the saltwater boils. Hannah, who was cavorting around in red cotton shorts, giggled inexplicably when I strode up the gangplank wearing much the same.

'Tell us of the lakes and the Torrible Zone,' demanded Tom, 'and the hills of the Chankly Bore.'

I was happy to be back on the boat. It gets to you like that. I had travelled on foot and in cars and trucks, and even once in a bus, but none of these conveyances made such marvellous use of the wind, that glorious resource that girdles the planet and takes you wherever you want to go, if you happen to have the skills and the time. And I hadn't been ready yet to leave my shipmates.

I could tell by the warmth of their welcome that everyone felt the same. We needed these few extra days onboard to take proper leave of each other and, most of all, of Hirta. So we hoisted the sails and sheeted them in, and again felt that thrill as the old boat shuddered with the wind and plunged her bow to the sea for this, my last trip in her. We could have gone anywhere, but Newport Rhode Island was where we headed. The Americas Cup was taking place there and, although the world's wealthiest millionaires strutting their stuff held little appeal, Tom made a living out of yachting journalism and reckoned there would be a story or two to be had.

And then, Tom said, we would go on to Mystic Seaport: 'A true sailor's port, with sailing museums and shrines and old boats.' It seemed a good and fitting place to leave *Hirta*, the crew and the sea. I phoned Ana with the news. I was on my way home.

EPILOGUE

FOWEY IS AS PRETTY AS A PLACE CAN BE, the perfect Cornish harbour town with steep, wooded hills tumbling down to the still waters of its estuary. In the autumn, after I came back from the Americas, Ana and I drove there from Sussex to spend a weekend with Patrick and his family. We had a notion about moving that way and starting again with the sheep, although in truth I was having a hard job wrenching my mind back from the sea. My brain seemed to have been so addled by salt water that it teemed with boats and nautical allusions.

As we breasted the ridge above the harbour town, I was expounding a pet theory to Ana, that being an island race we have the sea embedded in our very language.

'Take the phrase "To the bitter end",' I told her. 'You'd think it meant the conclusion of something pretty negative and drawn out but – hah! – no, it doesn't. The bitt, you see is a post for fastening the rope on a ship, so when you reach the bitter end it means the rope is all played out. Amazing, isn't it?'

A silence. Ana ignored me pointedly. Indeed, she stayed a bit quiet until she was introduced to Patrick's wife, Rosemary, and immediately recognised a fellow sufferer at the hands of the returned seadog, the trans-oceanic bore.

Ana was normally tolerant of my ways – after a few years of living with a person like me, you learn to make allowances – but I fear that this time my new obsession was getting beyond a joke. Perhaps I really was insufferable. I'm told I would walk with a roll, with what I took to be a sea-going sort of a gait, pepper my speech with nautical metaphors and would sigh at the merest thought of the sea.

Over breakfast of beans and eggs it occurred to Patrick that we might want to take his dinghy for a sail – 'She's small, but she'll give you a feel of the wind and the water,' he said. I looked across the table at Ana.

'Come on,' I cajoled her. 'You'll see what I've been going on about. It'll be a really nice morning's sail.'

'It might be nice for you,' she replied, 'but I think it looks extremely unappetising out there. Besides, it's hardly very warm, is it?'

'You'll be in good hands,' Patrick assured her. 'Your man knows his stuff. He's a good man in a tight spot.'

This, from Patrick, was praise indeed. I strutted and preened a little and put a manly arm around my girlfriend's shoulder. 'If we only ever put to sea on a sunny day, then where on earth would we be? What would have become of our island race?' I insisted. This ought to give you some indication of just how bad things had become.

With untypical forbearance, Ana denied herself the obvious retort. 'Well, alright, if we must,' she said. 'We'll see what you've learned out on the high seas.'

Patrick took us down to the dock where he kept his neat little fibreglass dinghy and helped me prepare it for sea. It was the work of a few minutes – child's play after our Atlantic voyaging.

Ana, however, was wearing her womanly disapproval hat, the sort a woman wears when she can think of a dozen good reasons not to do a thing but knows you're going to do it anyway. But as we bounded across the wavelets of the sheltered harbour, the sheer exuberance of it all blew that expression away and she, too, was soon wreathed in smiles. I swelled a little with pleasure and pride as she smiled back at me, then I hardened up (which means here to turn towards the wind), tightened the sheet and ran closer to the wind.

We rocketed across the open water towards the yacht club, where, in spite of the coolness of the morning, a small group of yachty-looking coves stood gathered on the terrace. They were certainly dressed for the part, in dapper yachting caps and blazers and white ducks, sipping gin and tonics and scanning the water with a hand shielding the brow. I hardened up a little more and then, to my dismay, realised that we were heading fast for the rocks beneath the terrace. 'READY ABOUT?' I yelled.

'What on earth do you mean by that?' asked Ana. She stared at me in amazement, as if I'd shouted something mildly distasteful.

'It's what you say when you're going to go about,' I explained quickly, with one eye on the rocks racing towards us. 'I say, "Ready about?" and then "Lee Ho," and...'

'Why can't you just say, "We're going to turn now," like you did in Greece?'

'Because it's not so concise and it's open to misinterpretation and also it's not what you're supposed to say... right? And we'd better make this snappy now; the shit's about to hit the fan. READY ABOUT?'

'Alright,' Ana said begrudgingly. (Although "Ready about?" is in fact a rhetorical question and as such does not require an answer.)

'LEE HO,' I howled and whipped the tiller over.

'What the...!' yelled Ana as the boom slammed across and smacked her hard on the ear. The boat tipped over, quick as a bucket, leaving Ana and me flailing about, half in and half out of the water. Thus discomposed, I lost control of the tiller and the boat kept on coming round.

'LET GO THE SHEETS!' I shouted.

'WHAT SHEETS?' Ana shouted straight back.

Then the wind burst into the sail on the other side and, with all our weight on the wrong side, we rolled into the water and the boat on top of us.

'Bugger!' I burbled as the icy water closed over my head. I scrabbled my way out from beneath the sail and scanned the water for my girlfriend.

Before long she bobbed to the surface and we clung together to the upturned hull. I looked sheepishly over at her. She shook the water out of her hair and spat out a mouthful of sea. 'I knew this was going to happen,' she said and nodded towards her wrist. 'Look, I even left my watch behind.'

And as she said this she smiled – a big, broad, watery smile over the upturned bottom of the boat – and then laughed out loud. It was a moment of epiphany for me. This is a most singular woman, I thought to myself. There she is down on her beam ends, bobbing about in the water, and she's laughing. The more I thought about it, the more I liked the cut of her jib.

The Jumblies

THE JUMBLIES

BY EDWARD LEAR

I

They went to sea in a Sieve, they did,
In a Sieve they went to sea:
In spite of all their friends could say,
On a winter's morn, on a stormy day,
In a Sieve they went to sea!
And when the Sieve turned round and round,
And every one cried, 'You'll all be drowned!'
They called aloud, 'Our Sieve ain't big,
But we don't care a button! We don't care a fig!
In a Sieve we'll go to sea!'
Far and few, far and few,
Are the lands where the Jumblies live;
Their heads are green, and their hands are blue,
And they went to sea in a Sieve.

II

They sailed away in a Sieve, they did,
In a Sieve they sailed so fast,

With only a beautiful pea-green veil
Tied with a riband by way of a sail,
To a small tobacco-pipe mast;
And every one said, who saw them go,
'O won't they be soon upset, you know!
For the sky is dark, and the voyage is long,
And happen what may, it's extremely wrong
In a Sieve to sail so fast!'
Far and few, far and few,
Are the lands where the Jumblies live;
Their heads are green, and their hands are blue,
And they went to sea in a Sieve.

III
The water it soon came in, it did,
The water it soon came in;
So to keep them dry, they wrapped their feet
In a pinky paper all folded neat,
And they fastened it down with a pin.
And they passed the night in a crockery-jar,
And each of them said, 'How wise we are!
Though the sky be dark, and the voyage be long,
Yet we never can think we were rash or wrong,
While round in our Sieve we spin!'
Far and few, far and few,
Are the lands where the Jumblies live;
Their heads are green, and their hands are blue,
And they went to sea in a Sieve.

IV

And all night long they sailed away;
And when the sun went down,
They whistled and warbled a moony song
To the echoing sound of a coppery gong,
In the shade of the mountains brown.
'O Timballo! How happy we are,
When we live in a Sieve and a crockery-jar,
And all night long in the moonlight pale,
We sail away with a pea-green sail,
In the shade of the mountains brown!'
Far and few, far and few,
Are the lands where the Jumblies live;
Their heads are green, and their hands are blue,
And they went to sea in a Sieve.

V

They sailed to the Western Sea, they did,
To a land all covered with trees,
And they bought an Owl, and a useful Cart,
And a pound of Rice, and a Cranberry Tart,
And a hive of silvery Bees.
And they bought a Pig, and some green Jack-daws,
And a lovely Monkey with lollipop paws,
And forty bottles of Ring-Bo-Ree,
And no end of Stilton Cheese.
Far and few, far and few,
Are the lands where the Jumblies live;

Their heads are green, and their hands are blue,
And they went to sea in a Sieve.

VI
And in twenty years they all came back,
In twenty years or more,
And every one said, 'How tall they've grown!
For they've been to the Lakes, and the Torrible Zone,
And the hills of the Chankly Bore!'
And they drank their health, and gave them a feast
Of dumplings made of beautiful yeast;
And every one said, 'If we only live,
We too will go to sea in a Sieve—
To the hills of the Chankly Bore!'
Far and few, far and few,
Are the lands where the Jumblies live;
Their heads are green, and their hands are blue,
And they went to sea in a Sieve.

from Edward Lear's *A Book of Nonsense*